# THE FEAR
# OF MONEY

BY
DANIEL J. CELIA

FOREWORD BY: DR. WOODROW KROLL

Intermedia Publishing Group

## The Fear of Money

Published by:
Intermedia Publishing, Inc.
P.O. Box 2825
Peoria, Arizona 85380
www.intermediapub.com

ISBN 978-1-937654-56-6

Printed in the United States of America

Editors: Yvonne Celia and Janet Battaglia

This book has been made available in cooperation with American Family Association and available at www.afastore.afa.net

# THE FEAR
# OF MONEY

*In appreciation to:*
*American Family Association and their unwavering*
*commitment to Our Lord and Savior, our country and*
*helping to restore the Moral fiber of America.*


*And to*
*Dr. Woodrow Kroll and Back to the Bible*
*For Calling America Back to the Bible*


*I am most Thankful to the Lord. His grace to me is*
*overwhelming and His gift to me of my wife, children, and*
*grandchildren is a true blessing straight from Him.*

# FOREWORD
## BY: Dr. Woodrow Kroll

Are you afraid of money? If you said no, read on. If you said yes, read on. If you don't know for sure, definitely read on.

Often when people are asked if they're afraid of money they shoot back, "Yeah. I'm afraid I won't have enough of it." That's not just a glib answer; that's a reality.

Napoleon Hill wrote a book entitled *Think and Grow Rich* in 1937 during the Great Depression. At the time of Hill's death in 1970, *Think and Grow Rich* had sold twenty million copies. It remains a perennial best-seller after seventy-five years. *Business Week Magazine's Best-Seller List* ranked *Think and Grow Rich* as the sixth best-selling paperback business book of all time. John Maxwell placed T*hink and Grow Rich* on his *Lifetime "Must Read" Books List.*

While *Think and Grow Rich* is a motivational book on how to have a successful life, it basically teaches the steps to high achievement and financial independence.

So why is Napoleon Hill's best-selling book important to the question of whether or not we fear money? Because in it the author lists "The Six Basic Fears" that people experience and number one—the fear of poverty—he says is "the most destructive fear" of all. I would agree, but for different reasons than those proposed by Napoleon Hill.

As I watch from my little window on the world, people often fear money in three questioning ways:  1) what if I don't have enough of it? 2) if I do have enough, what should I do with it? and, 3) if I have more than I need, what should I do with the excess?

Believe it or not, for the majority of you reading this book, these questions are listed in inverse order of reality. Even during economic hard times, more people need to answer question three than question two, and more need to answer question two than question one.

In the pages that follow, Dan Celia addresses our fear of money from a biblical perspective, from years of personal experience in helping others overcome their fears, and from a heart that genuinely wants you to handle what God entrusts to you in faith, not fear.

Throughout this book you will see challenging themes surfacing again and again, such as: it's not what you have but what you do with what you have that's important; our attitudes toward money are often more reflective of Satan's schemes than of God's stewardship; our focus on present need often blinds us to the blessing of future reward.

There is an antidote to fear, even our fear of money. That antidote is faith. Someone has wisely said, "Fear knocked on the door. Faith answered. And there was no one there."

If we can learn to trust God to provide for our basic needs, if we can understand from His Word what to do with the resources He entrusts to us, and if we can muster the courage to become heavenly minded in all that we have in life and all that we are, we will be inoculated from living in fear with the life-saving gift of living in faith.

As you read the pages that follow, wrestle with these thoughts about faith from God's Word:

"O woman, great is your faith!
Let it be to you as you desire" (Matt. 15:28).

"Why are you so fearful? How is it that you have no faith?"
(Mark 4:40)

"Go your way; your faith has made you well"
(Mark 10:52).

"Have faith in God" (Mark 22:22).

"And the apostles said to the Lord, 'Increase our faith'"
(Luke 17:5).

"I have prayed for you, that your faith should not fail"
(Luke 22:32).

"The just shall live by faith" (Rom. 1:17).

"Whatever is not from faith is sin" (Rom. 14:23).

"So then those who are of faith are blessed..." (Gal. 3:9).

As you read the very practical and poignant advice in the chapters that follow, Dan Celia will frequently speak of the "focus of our heart." I know his desire is not that you think and grow rich. His desire is that you have faith and grow rich in the kingdom of God. It doesn't just make a world of difference. It makes an eternity of difference.

Dr. Woodrow Kroll, President
Back to the Bible International

# Table of Contents

# Preface
# **A Message for Today**

Dear Friend,

Have you ever considered that we spend at least half of our waking hours working to earn a living? In fact, for many of us, that percentage is probably significantly higher. Now, it is good to be thankful that God has provided us with some wonderful opportunities to earn a living, but many of us may not always work in a job that we particularly love. Out of a desire to provide for our family and be a contributing member of society, we endure often stressful and tedious days, weeks, and even months, doing whatever we have the opportunity to do. Work can be highly rewarding but is also frequently a considerable challenge. So, we see that whether we have our dream job, or are working toward that end, the paycheck we receive represents a significant percentage of our life's effort.

Many of us know that we are to do all things unto Christ and should have this attitude of gratefulness that we have decent jobs and rewarding work to do. If you've browsed my website, or listened to any of my talks, you know one of the most prominent themes I discuss is that the Lord provides for us, even when we're not entirely considerate of Him, nor grateful (nor even aware sometimes.) So if the Lord truly considers us of much greater value than a sparrow in the field, and He feeds the sparrows who don't even work, why is money one of the most crippling stressors on the planet?

The answer is simple. We have a deep fear of money.

That may seem counter-intuitive, since we are led to believe that we are more likely to be prone to loving money. But the truth is, we never feel we have enough money, because *we fear it*. Think about it—we have fear about the money we have earned each week. There is the fear of not making enough, the fear of losing it, perhaps the fear of whether we are investing it properly, or maybe the fear of not getting rid of our debt. Fear pervades most of our thoughts about money.

However, all through Scripture we are called not to fear but to put our trust in the Lord in all things that we do. I have found in over twenty-five years of counseling individuals and organizations about the stewardship of their money, we are usually very good at "trusting the Lord"—until it comes to our money. We have somehow managed to compartmentalize our money away from, or out of the responsibility of God. We take that responsibility upon ourselves and often leave the Lord out of the picture. But He commands us not to worry about money. Worry is rooted in fear. As I've explained, when you break it down, that paycheck represents the hours you've worked. The sweat that's poured. The stress you've endured. The focus you've maintained. Day in and day out. You trust the Lord in your daily effort, and money is simply a representative of that effort. So this book is about taking it that one step further and trusting Him with the *symbol* of that effort, namely money.

I truly believe that when you apply the principles in this book, you will learn to overcome this fear. You will walk day by day, trusting the Lord in all of your circumstances and opportunities, with all that you have, and knowing it is God in whom you place your trust.

**- Dan Celia**

*"Therefore I say to you, do not worry about your life, what you will eat or what you will drink; nor about your body, what you will put on. Is not life more than food and the body more than clothing? 26 Look at the birds of the air, for they neither sow nor reap nor gather into barns; yet your heavenly Father feeds them. Are you not of more value than they? 27 Which of you by worrying can add one cubit to his stature?*

*28 "So why do you worry about clothing? Consider the lilies of the field, how they grow: they neither toil nor spin; 29 and yet I say to you that even Solomon in all his glory was not arrayed like one of these. 30 Now if God so clothes the grass of the field, which today is, and tomorrow is thrown into the oven, will He not much more clothe you, O you of little faith?*

*31 "Therefore do not worry, saying, 'What shall we eat?' or 'What shall we drink?' or 'What shall we wear?' 32 For after all these things the Gentiles seek. For your heavenly Father knows that you need all these things. 33 But seek first the kingdom of God and His righteousness, and all these things shall be added to you. [34] Therefore do not worry about tomorrow, for tomorrow will worry about its own things. Sufficient for the day is its own trouble.'* **Matthew 6:25-34**

# Chapter One

# Born Into the Fear Of Money

My wife of thirty-two years is one of eleven children. She falls in the middle of that pack and, needless to say, there are close to one hundred grandchildren and great-grandchildren. As a result, I have had many opportunities to be around little ones. I always notice that, even at a very young age, money is extremely important to even the smallest child. They don't fully understand what is behind it, nor do they fully understand the power of it, but they learn to protect it and even to hoard it. They will save money and grow it and intuitively understand that the more you have each month, the better job you have done and the more you have to be proud of. They also learn to want more of it.

Of course when we are raised with that attitude, as so many parents teach their children, we naturally grow up with the idea that more is better and we need to protect our money at all costs. Sometimes the last thing we want to do is to spend it, because when we spend it, we diminish our stockpile and that can't be a good thing. But is that truly the way to insure we have more than enough money? Scripture teaches us otherwise.

My wife and I have taught our children from the first babysitting dollar they ever earned that they needed to *tithe* to the church or to Kingdom work with that money. With each child tithing became as natural as bathing and just as children grow up learning to earn money or save it, to hoard it or spend it, our children grew up intuitively understanding the habit of giving. Today, as my children are married and on their own, they have a very different perspective of their money than others their age. They care very little about what they have, and place little value on material possessions, but they always have enough and even more than enough. My wife and I are obviously very glad for their financial peace and are highly grateful for their attitudes. You know, when you learn that giving is a priority, the value of money in one's life changes dramatically. The Bible speaks very clearly about our money and the attitude that we should have toward it. I particularly like the parable in Luke 12, where Jesus is speaking to His disciples.

*'16 Then He spoke a parable to them, saying: "The ground of a certain rich man yielded plentifully. 17 And he thought within himself, saying, 'What shall I do, since I have no room to store my crops?' 18 So he said, 'I will do this: I will pull down my barns and build greater, and there I will store all my crops and my goods. 19 And I will say to my soul, "Soul, you have many goods laid up for many years; take your ease; eat, drink, and be merry."' 20 But God said to him, 'Fool! This night your soul will be required of you; then whose will those things be which you have provided?'*

*21 "So is he who lays up treasure for himself, and is not rich toward God." 22 Then He said to His disciples, "Therefore I say to you, do not worry about your life, what you will eat; nor about the body, what you will put on. 23 Life is more than food, and the body is more than clothing. 24 Consider the ravens, for they neither sow nor reap, which have neither storehouse nor barn; and God feeds them. Of how much more value are you than the birds? 25 And which of you by worrying can add one cubit to his stature? 26 If you then are not able to do the least, why are you anxious for the rest? 27 Consider the lilies, how they grow: they neither toil nor spin; and yet I say to you, even Solomon in all his glory was not arrayed like one of these. 28 If then God so clothes the grass, which today is in the field and tomorrow is thrown into the oven, how much more will He clothe you, O you of little faith?*

*29 "And do not seek what you should eat or what you should drink, nor have an anxious mind. 30 For all these things the nations of the world seek after, and your Father knows that you need these things. 31 But seek the kingdom of God, and all these things [a] shall be added to you.*

*32 "Do not fear, little flock, for it is your Father's good pleasure to give you the kingdom. 33 Sell what you have and give alms; provide yourselves money bags which do not grow old, a treasure in the heavens that does not fail, where no thief approaches nor moth destroys. 34 For where your treasure is, there your heart will be also.'*
**Luke 12:16-34**

The frightening aspect of this parable is that it begins with God Himself calling this man a fool. Now, for most of us, you would think this would be enough to cause us to change our attitudes about laying up treasures for ourselves or hoarding. The other important lesson in this parable to note is that as we continue to hoard, we continue to worry. Fear of losing money or fear of not having enough begins to set in. Just look at the rest of the parable. The Lord is calling us not to worry. There are a number of verses in that parable that stand out to me. Most of our fear comes from the fact that we worry, yet in verse 23 Jesus clearly points out that life is more than food and the body is more than clothing. He reminds us how He provides for the least in the earthly realm, so He will certainly continue to provide for us as long as we work hard and follow His will. We do not need to build bigger barns and warehouses and storehouses so that we might have plenty.

In order for us to get comfortable enough to move away from this fear of losing the money we have, we need to understand some very important pieces of Scripture. To be good stewards over what God has given us and to get rid of the fear and worry about tomorrow, one of the most important—if not the most important verse—in this parable is verse 34: *'For where your treasure is, there your heart will be also.'*

You know, there are many successful salesmen who use that very line (although they don't know it) as part of their propaganda to get people to buy or invest in certain things. Human nature is such that our hearts are filled with covetousness. As a successful sales coach teaches, we may think we don't like to be sold on something, but we love to buy! We desire what our neighbor has and what others have.

How many of us have sat in front of a news reel and watched how some billionaire is giving away millions of dollars, or growing their fortune, or living in what could be considered a "castle" and we have envied. Have we not said, "Oh, what I could do if I had that!" You see, again, human nature is such that our hearts will lust after those things that we truly desire. We have this desire to get everything that we want, but not necessarily need. We do not have a "want" to be grateful that God has fulfilled our needs. Because of this simple truth, we are constantly stressed over growing our money, protecting what we have, having the ability to earn, being able to save, and to pay for our children's education. All the while, God has the full intention of giving us the desires of our hearts— as long as those desires are not above our relationship with our Lord.

Jesus knew all too well the desires of our hearts. He knew very well that our hearts were full of fleshly lusts, covetousness, and those things we would desire but not necessarily need. I believe, as I read through Scripture, that Jesus also knows the vast majority of those things would have something to do with money—with treasures. I think if that were not the case, He would not speak so much about the issue of our worshipping the very thing that is not ours, and that instead of trying to hoard more, we should and would be giving it away.

It is my firm belief that the ability to remove our fear of money, or our fear of *losing* money, has a lot to do with changing the *desires of our hearts*. Unfortunately, that comes with a price; the price of dramatically impacting our ego and our pride, as a man or a woman. After all, what will people think if we simply go through life fulfilling our *needs* and not *wanting* anything more than what God provides? The Joneses might whisper that we're not *able* to hoard treasure, or the Smiths might snicker that we have a slightly outdated TV. Heaven forbid!

I believe many people are like I was. I grew up in a dysfunctional household. My mother, whom I loved dearly, was deaf and also a chronic alcoholic. My father was seldom home. He worked three jobs on a regular basis. Growing up, I cannot remember my father saying more than one sentence to me at a time, and it was usually something relatively negative. We had no conversations that a father and son would desire to have, except when I worked for him. My father was a painting contractor and I was often called in to work on various projects with him. Any conversations we then had were work-related.

While we were growing up, it was obvious that my brother was going to be the successful one. Incidentally, my brother was a chronic drug addict and died in a state prison a few years ago. I was expected to amount to nothing. When I left the military, my desire was for only one thing— to be financially successful. This was not because I wanted riches, rather it was to prove to those around me (particularly my family) that I was capable of being successful. I truly worshipped money. I worshipped success. I worshipped ego and I worshipped pride. I once heard a successful NFL wide-receiver give his testimony. He was talking about his life before he accepted the Lord, as he was about to commit suicide. He blamed everything on his ego. He said that EGO stands for Edging God Out. I don't know that I edged God out. I believe that I never really had any God to edge out. My God was success. My God was work and I sometimes worked 24/7 for weeks at a time. My treasure was success.

I say all of that because I believe a lot of people— particularly men—are driven by the same things. They are driven by ego and pride. Do they know that they don't need a big house or a $40,000 car? I believe we know that deep down, but rather than talk about ourselves, we allow our "things" to show just how successful we have become. This idea of changing our hearts, so that our treasures would be heavenly bound, and we would be heavenly minded is a very difficult thing to do when so many of us have a mindset of worshipping the very thing that could ultimately destroy our everlasting life.

So, where do we begin to try to change the focus of our heart? So many people ask me about stewardship. I speak all over the country and host a national radio call-in program on over 400 stations and from this, I get hundreds of e-mails each week asking about financial stewardship. The primary question people want answered is how to guard, protect, and invest their money. To a degree, this is what my ministry is all about; to help people do the right thing and perhaps, more importantly, to keep them from doing the wrong thing with what God has given them. But the key to financial peace is the reason I'm writing this book. We need to change the focus of our hearts, and that in turn frees us to be infinitely wiser with our money.

So, how *can* we get our hearts focused on the right things, when all the while we have ministries such as mine telling people that they need to invest their money correctly? Keep reading, and I'll show you.

## Chapter Two

# Money Represents Your Life Effort

In chapter one, I hinted at how money is a primitive representative of your life's effort. I want to explore that a little more, because understanding this concept is the key to understanding the deeper concept of why your money is part of your life, and why it is necessary to lay down our *entire life* before God in order to see His power work in our lives to bring not only financial peace, but a much larger, lasting peace.

> *'16 Then He spoke a parable to them, saying: "The ground of a certain rich man yielded*

*plentifully. 17 And he thought within himself, saying, 'What shall I do, since I have no room to store my crops?' 18 So he said, 'I will do this: I will pull down my barns and build greater, and there I will store all my crops and my goods. 19 And I will say to my soul, "Soul, you have many goods laid up for many years; take your ease; eat, drink, and be merry."' 20 But God said to him, 'Fool! This night your soul will be required of you; then whose will those things be which you have provided?' 21 "So is he who lays up treasure for himself, and is not rich toward God."'* **Luke 12:16-21**

This parable is quite obviously a commentary on both greed and laziness. First, notice that it was God who blessed the man. His ground yielded an abundant harvest. So abundant that he would have had to build bigger barns (plural) to store all of it. This man was freely given much by the Lord, but wanted to hoard it for selfish reasons. He didn't want to work for many years. These things within the man's heart are counter to the scriptural model of being productive. We are instructed in numerous places in Scripture (Old Testament and New) to be constantly, or continuously fruitful. Fruitfulness in this particular parable would have been sharing his abundant harvest with the poor, which would have insured an even greater blessing in the man's future because Proverbs 28:27 says, *"He who gives to the poor will not lack, But he who hides his eyes will have many curses."*

Notice what God says at the end of the Scripture in Luke: *'Fool! This night your soul will be required of you; then whose will those things be which you have provided?'* There is a critical clue in that line. God required the man's life because he did not honor the Lord with his harvest. This is related to Proverbs 28:27—the man's harvest, or his crop is the result of the energy he's put into tilling the ground, sowing the seeds, and harvesting the crop. God brought the abundant increase, but the man thought it was his effort that made the crop grow. A good portion of a man's life is represented by the symbol of his harvest. In this parable, a harvest is an excellent metaphor to use because it covers any type of labor, whether it be the service industry, retail, banking, construction, or in fact, farmers. The harvest in many cases is our paycheck, but it could be an unexpected bonus, interest we didn't know we were accruing, the value of our house increasing when we didn't expect it, and other such things. The point is that we work, but God provides our jobs, and any increase we gain.

So, would it be reasonable to conclude that God gives us our very life, provides work for us (because work is rewarding for more than just the paycheck) and then provides the increase from our labor? I believe it is entirely reasonable. To take it a step further, I conclude we are simply stewards of what God has given us.

So then, as I said in chapter one, the critical factor is the focus of our heart. If we focus our hearts on relying upon the simple representation of our life effort, doesn't that seem like a very primitive, narrow approach to security? It really does. I would add that it is a very difficult way to security, and in fact will enslave you. It is infinitely easier being a steward. Why? Because the responsibility to produce is removed from your shoulders! If God brings the increase, and we're simply living our lives from a "top-down" approach by taking care of the focus of our heart, then we're trusting Him with our entire life, right? We do this by realizing that money is simply a symbol of the effort of our life, and we've given our life to Him. We've dedicated our life to God but we can undo much of that dedication by not trusting Him with our money. When we shift our mindset to understanding the truth in the Word—that we're simply stewards of the life God has given us, and as a result stewards of the money God has given us, the *fear* of money is removed.

"How do we shift our mindset?" you may ask. I'll explain. As stewards, we undoubtedly have a responsibility to do the right thing with the "nuts and bolts" questions of how to invest and protect the money God has given us. Our stewardship responsibility, however, is meaningless if we do not understand one of the fundamental truths that the Bible gives us in reference to our faith.

Let's look at 1 Corinthians 4:1-2:

> *'1 Let a man so consider us, as servants of Christ and stewards of the mysteries of God. 2 Moreover it is required in stewards that one be found faithful.'*

This Scripture is the foundational verse of my ministry. Here Paul is reminding us that, as we come to know the Lord and are believers, our first stewardship responsibility is toward the sacred mysteries of God, or the gospel of Jesus Christ. In fact, we cannot even begin a journey on stewardship, or release the fear of losing what God has given us, without understanding that first and foremost we have a responsibility to be a *faithful* steward of the gospel.

If we have this foundational truth embedded in us as the primary desire of our hearts, then everything that we do in life—not only the management of our finances—will relate to proclaiming and protecting the sacred mysteries of God. I know that we cannot all be preachers, teachers, evangelists, and missionaries, but we are all called to work hard at being a steward of the Gospel. One of the ways through which I believe God calls us to do that is with our finances. If we have learned only one thing about this government over the past years, we have learned that there is no way on God's green earth that society in general (at least the minority of our society who seem to drive *everything* that happens in Washington) is ever going to allow Washington to support those tenets of the Christian faith. We will never see government money going to churches to insure that they are proclaiming the Gospel and keeping their doors open. We are not going to see the government supporting missionaries, so they can stay on the mission fields to reach the ends of the earth with the Gospel. The government will certainly not make sure that evangelistic services of today are going to be financially supported, so that people can come to the saving knowledge of God's grace. They are not going to insure that Christian conservative talk radio and even Christian music stations will be able to stay on the air, proclaiming the Gospel. Christian television will always have difficulty growing because of finances, and certainly the government will not provide for those networks to get on the air and stay on the air. *It is up to you and me.* We don't have to like it, but Paul reminds us that we really have no choice. As believers in our Lord and Savior, the fact remains we have no choice but to come to the understanding that we must support the work of God.

I believe passionately that we all need to be soldiers of Christ. I am sure you all know someone, or perhaps you yourself who were in the military. I distinctly remember a company commander getting in my face, reminding me that I had no mind and that my decisions did not matter nor did my opinions matter; the only thing that mattered was the mission given to me by my commanding officer. His mission becomes my mission. His opinions become my opinions. My work becomes only what is set before me by my commanding officer. Oh, if we could only have that attitude when it comes to being Christians. As faithful soldiers of Christ, He is our Commanding Officer. We can say that Christ came to earth to do many things and we can try to go through the New Testament and come up with all kinds of fluffy reasons why Christ came. What He said Himself however, on numerous occasions, is that He primarily came to seek and save the lost. That would be us. All of us. He died and rose again so that we, the lost, could come to the cross and have eternal life and salvation.

I know we all get caught up at times wondering what our true purpose is in this life and what God's intention might be for us. I know that we get concerned in our thinking and may ask questions like, "What are my gifts?" "Do I even have any gifts?" or "What would God want me to do in a certain situation?" Believe this—one thing that we all have in common as soldiers of Christ is to follow the orders and follow in the footsteps of our Commanding Officer. Jesus Christ came to seek and save the lost. As faithful servants of Christ, we need to do nothing less than to seek and save the lost. This means that in all we are doing, whether it is teaching Sunday school, being on the mission field, preaching, teaching, evangelizing, or just doing our everyday job—we should be endeavoring to seek and save the lost. I know some of you may not like this, but this is true for our money as well. All we have and do needs to work toward the purpose of seeking and saving the lost. That is ultimately being a good steward of the mysteries of God, and how we should biblically approach not only our finances, but our work, social interactions, and anything else we spend time doing. Our entire life is what we honor God with, and if money represents a portion of our life effort, then we must honor God with our money to this end as well or we're instantly excluding a large portion of our life's commitment to God.

Notice where in 1 Corinthians 4:2 [Emphasis added] Paul says, *'Moreover, it is required in stewards (that's you and me) that one would be found faithful,'* so that we might hear those words *'Well done, good and faithful servant'* (Matt. 25:21). I remember early in my Christian walk being deeply struck by those verses, which is why this is the pivotal verse of my ministry. I earnestly desire to do my best and hear those words some day. I remember coming to the conclusion that, whether I liked it or not, my gifts in the effort of seeking and saving the lost were in finance. I remember telling my wife one day, many years ago, "I don't want this ministry. I don't want to be doing what I am doing. I want to do more. I want to go on the mission field. I want to preach and I want to teach. I want to have an impact. I want to be in the trenches. I want to have an impact for the Kingdom." I came to the realization that I could remember what some company stocks sold for three years ago or what corn and cattle futures were selling for and what the price of oil is on any given day, right off the top of my head. Then I was sad to consider that sometimes I can't remember the verses I read this morning during my devotions. I realized however, that God was smacking me across the head saying, "Your gift is here. You need to use it for the Kingdom."

Regarding our specific gifts, we all need to come to a similar conclusion at some point in time. When it comes to our financial stewardship, however, we must know that under *all* circumstances, we are called to be stewards of the Gospel. And I can tell you it is truly amazing how your life will dramatically change for the better when you develop that as a desire of your heart.

Now down to those nuts and bolts again. Certainly, one of the things about which we are most afraid is the turmoil and turbulence that comes if we do not have enough dollars to fulfill—not only our needs, wants and desires—but also our obligations to the debtor. There is a fear each day that circumstances could change and so we must hold a little back. Sometimes, even at the peril of not giving to Kingdom work, we hoard and save for that rainy day when turbulence may strike. And this mindset usually leads to worry and stress *every* day of our lives. Yes, we should save for our emergency fund, but the fact that we are saving for that should relieve the stress. By the way, saving is different than hoarding.

The fear of money, however, is easy to put aside, along with the worry and stress it can cause. To do this, we must become focused and committed to the treasure that is in our hearts. The only investment which is absolutely secure and the only investment that is a sure thing is the investment we make in the Kingdom. Believe me when I say that. I've seen a lot, done a lot, had no money, had more than enough money and it ultimately comes down to what we do for the Kingdom that brings security and peace. It is not the financial investments we make otherwise.

The difficult part, of course, is dealing with our ego, pride, and all those things that have been ingrained in our minds for so long which keep our hearts from being focused on the true treasure. Do you remember Jesus as He was in the boat with His apostles in Matthew chapter eight? He was fast asleep in the midst of a storm—a storm which the disciples certainly believed was going to overtake them. They frantically woke Him, asking *"Save us, for we are perishing."* It is hard to imagine the Lord's tone of voice—whether it was one of compassion or one of "Oh brother, here we go again." I believe He may have teasingly smiled and said, *"Why are you fearful, oh you of little faith?"* We often fear the loss of money, or the loss of our job or ability to continue to work—*before* the turmoil has even struck. Even in the *midst* of the turmoil, however, I am sure the Lord would turn to us, smile and say the same thing. Perhaps the concern for our "dollars" is not a legitimate concern. We should have enough to provide for our family. But, could it rather be a lack of faith? Let that sink in for a minute.

I don't want to accuse anyone of having a lack of faith, but the truth is that when we take our eyes off of Jesus, like Peter in the middle of another storm in the middle of a lake, we *will* begin to sink. I don't think this could ever be truer than in our financial lives, or in the way that we conduct ourselves as we attempt to walk with the Lord. The question that Jesus asked of those in the boat was, "Why are you fearful, oh you of little faith?" Here was a group of men that were walking daily with the Lord, and they had seen the miracles that He was performing. I hope by now they had come to the conclusion that this truly was the Son of God, and indeed was God Himself. How is it possible that they could be fearful? Well, pretty easily, and I think we can all relate to this. Like Peter, we simply take our eyes off Him and start to drown in the circumstances around us. It also often seems that as one storm subsides, another picks up. When one is over, another one comes stronger than ever. But Jesus rebuked the storms and they instantly ceased. It is all about what our eyes are consistently focused on. And regarding money, this comes down to being faithful toward the Kingdom work as we have discussed.

C.S. Lewis said that our sorrows, as Christians, should be regarded as superficial. I believe this is true of our circumstances, which may be coming by way of a storm or turmoil. This should be superficial to us. Yes, we have to deal with it. Yes, it may be obvious and evident in our lives. Yes, we must pray for discernment and how to deal with it and work through it in the best way we possibly can, but we must also analyze whether this storm or current circumstances may have been created by a poor choice that we made somewhere along the line. Perhaps these are just a set of unforeseen circumstances that are a result of somebody else's bad choice. Nevertheless, even in the midst of it, as we deal with it, it should be relatively superficial because we are either growing in wisdom, or God will reward us for enduring suffering in love, even when it is caused by another's injustice toward us.

These storms should not occupy every waking hour to the point we take our eyes off Jesus. They should not occupy our life to the point we begin to wallow in self-pity, and forget to take joy in the glory of God. If we continue to get caught up in our self-pity, we will very quickly change the desires of our heart. We will change the treasures that we seek, and we may even change what we worship. It really is about faith and how we deal with the circumstances. When catastrophe hits and calamity seems to shake our world, this is the time to put feet to our faith and to fall deeper into the boat; not to wake the Lord up in fear, but perhaps to move closer to Him, knowing that all is okay when we are that much closer to Him.

I remember God making a major change in my life at the end of 2009. I had lost a major sponsor of my radio ministry, and a pastor friend of mine said to me, "Why are you fearful? You desire to do what is right in the eyes of God, and you are setting forth to do it. He will bless that, so why are you fearful?" In one month—the month of January 2010—the money that I was so fearful of losing (after a long sponsorship) came back to me with a surplus, so that our ministry could not just limp along, but continue on stronger than ever. I had to be reminded that we need to *always* do what is right in the sight of God. We shouldn't strive to have a "little" faith, but to have *abundant* faith, that as our God has brought us to this place, and we continue to do His work and to honor and glorify Him in *everything we do*, we have nothing to fear—especially when it comes to our money.

# Chapter Three

# The Real Treasure

*'44 "Again, the kingdom of heaven is like treasure hidden in a field, which a man found and hid; and for joy over it he goes and sells all that he has and buys that field. 45 "Again, the kingdom of heaven is like a merchant seeking beautiful pearls, 46 who, when he had found one pearl of great price, went and sold all that he had and bought it.'*
**Matthew 13:44-46**

Now that we have spoken about money just being a symbol of our life's daily effort, I'd like to take a look at the Scripture above. If you haven't guessed yet, the Treasure and Pearl being spoken of in this parable, is Jesus Himself. The implied meaning here is that Jesus is so valuable; He is worth selling everything we have to gain Him.

Now of course, we know we don't have to sell anything to gain Christ, nor could we ever buy Him. What Jesus is saying here is that we will not be "short-changed" if we devote everything we do to Him. That's a tricky statement, though. Are we all to give up our jobs and enter the full-time ministry? As I said in a previous chapter, of course not—but we can give our life to Him, and put Him first in everything we do. The best way to do that is to get to know Him, and the more we get to know Him—an amazing thing happens—we become like Him. How do we get to know Him? Prayer, study of His word, and fellowship with those who love Him, too.

"What does this have to do with my money?" you may ask. Well, when you discover Jesus—and I'm talking about truly getting to know Him—you'll feel His presence in your heart, changing you day by day. Everything you do will be that much more Christ-like, and pretty soon you will be making a big difference for His kingdom—without even trying!

You see, what Jesus was talking about here was a matter of priorities. He's saying that if we only knew what He could do for us, we would *voluntarily* give up everything to gain

Him! And honestly, that is what we have to do. I know I've said you don't have to sell everything, and enter the full-time ministry—what God wants is actually *more* than that. He wants your heart, entirely. If you would be *willing* to sell everything and do whatever He wants you to, you're on the right track. But it takes time to know God's will for your life, and one of the easiest ways to test yourself, to see if you truly desire that Pearl of great price, is to see how willing you are to support His Kingdom with your money.

I want to draw your attention to something very interesting in the parable. Notice that in both examples, the men were searching for treasure. The man in the field didn't stumble upon the treasure accidentally—what was he doing in that field that didn't belong to him anyway? The merchant was searching, and searching for fine pearls. Believe me, jewelers in those days knew their craft, and to find a pearl that was worth everything this merchant had, would be a once in a lifetime find—a man might not even make that find once in a lifetime. The point is, these men were looking for treasure, and they knew its value when they found it.

Measure that up against your own life. Are you searching for an easy way to live? That one big deal that will put you ahead? Perhaps you believe it is the perfect job that will secure your future, or the right investment? Consider the pearl merchant; do you think if he was searching in the limestone quarries he would have found that pearl? Perhaps he might have even been looking at the oysters in the fish market for a few pearls. If he wasn't searching through troves and troves of specific pearl collections, there was very little chance he would have found that rare pearl that someone with less knowledge of the craft had overlooked.

The analogy to Jesus is obvious. You could sit in church your entire life and never really know Him. You have to search for Him, personally. You have to spend time trying to figure out why everything people say about Him is true. Does He change lives? Does He bring peace, love, and joy? How does He do that? You have to sacrifice time and effort seeking Him. That's when you find Him. I speak from experience. I was one of those people that pulled off the side of the road and accepted the Lord as a result of listening to Charles Stanley on the Radio. Trust me, He can and will change lives. God even tells us this much through the prophet Jeremiah:

> *' And you will seek Me and find Me, when*
> *you search for Me with all your heart.'*
> **Jeremiah 29:13**

This searching with all of your heart includes a willingness to do anything to find Him. Think about it; what if you could find a treasure that would completely change your life, but it required you undertake a very strenuous expedition. If you were guaranteed of finding this treasure—I know you would go after it. People undertake such treasure hunts without even a guarantee. They take out loans against their property, they buy excavating equipment, hire crews of diggers, and archaeologists, and set off to find great treasure. Some of them do. Most of them don't. God *guarantees* we will find Him, when we seek Him with all of our heart.

So what can you expect to find, when you find Jesus? In short, everything you need for the rest of your life. Take a look at the Old Testament names of God, with their inherent meaning:

**Yahweh:** Lord or Jehovah—connotation of absolute power

**Adonai:** Lord or Master—connotation of absolute power

**El Elyon:** The Most High God—stresses superiority to other so-called gods

**El Shaddai:** The Lord God Almighty—connotations of a Father who chastens in love

**Jehovah Nissi:** The Lord, My Banner—stresses that God is our rallying point and victory

**Jehovah-Raah:** The Lord, My Shepherd—stresses how intently God cares for His people

**Jehovah Rapha:** The Lord That Heals—stresses how God is our healer; physically, spiritually, and emotionally

**Jehovah Shammah:** The Lord Is There—Jesus said He would never leave us, nor forsake us

**Jehovah Tsidkenu:** The Lord Our Righteousness—Jesus died in our place, and through Him we are made righteous

**Jehovah Mekoddishkem:** The Lord Who Sanctifies You—the Lord cleanses us and sets us apart for His purposes

**El Olam:** The Everlasting God—stresses God's unchanging nature and his inexhaustible resources

**Jehovah Sabaoth:** The Lord of Hosts—stresses God as the military leader of Heaven's armies

**Jehovah Jireh:** The Lord Provides—stresses God's provision for His people

**Jehovah Shalom:** The Lord Is Peace

Wow! When you take a look at this list it's easy to see why the men in the parable would give up everything they had to gain the real Treasure. God made it very clear to His people that He would provide for them, in every way necessary. In John 16:33 He says, *'These things I have spoken to you, that in Me you may have peace. In the world you will have tribulation; but be of good cheer, I have overcome the world."* 'Our peace and provision is found in the person of Jesus Christ, the real Treasure. Through Him we inherit all the riches and blessings of Heaven. God promises us provision, but in order to appropriate these blessings, we need to gain Jesus, or know Him more and more personally every day. We inherit every single promise in the Bible the minute we make Jesus Lord of our life, but we may not even know what these promises are, so how can we walk in them, or appropriate them? We need to seek Him, and get to know Him. As we do this, our will shall be transformed into His will, and we will achieve things we could never have dreamed of, for His kingdom. And we will love every minute of it!

But what does it really take to experience this kind of life? Keep reading, and I'll show you.

# Chapter Four

# **Give It All to Christ**

That is an alarming title for a chapter! I'm sure that right away most of you are thinking, "Is he talking about my *money*? Am I to give it *all* away?" There is that fear again. See how quickly it crops up—but so you will continue to read on, know that this is *not* what I am talking about here. I am talking about our fear. I am talking about our work. I am talking about control of the things that occupy our minds, hearts, and desires each and every day. Anything that obscures us from seeking the real Treasure needs to be given to Christ.

We are not to separate or compartmentalize these things which are related to our money. If Jesus wants our whole heart, He wants exactly that. If we compartmentalize our money, our giving, or our debt in any way, we are not seeking Him with our whole heart.

Many of you have had an opportunity over the past few years to visit one of my town hall meetings. One thing I always make note of when I speak is that if you are a believer in Jesus Christ, you may be a person who prays for everything. It's no secret I believe prayer is a wonderful gift and something we should do throughout each day—but how often do we seem to pass over our financial situation. Or if we do, we simply pray for more money. We very seldom pray for who we can trust to help us with our finances. We don't pray for where we might give it. We don't pray for where we might spend it. We don't pray through the struggles, trials, and turbulence that lie ahead because of a lack of it. We always desire to take total control over this area of our lives, and we very seldom give it all to Christ.

Yet, we have to come to a place where we understand that we cannot have faith and continue to compartmentalize or separate our finances from that faith. This is something that has been going on throughout the history of time. It seems a whole lot easier to keep those financial areas separated from God. If we do that, we do not need to consult Him or to do His work. We can simply do whatever *we* are pleased to do, while not "bothering" God with the management of it. This is because we want total control.

I love Paul's rhetorical question in Romans 8:35:

> *'Who shall separate us from the love of Christ? Shall tribulation, or distress, or persecution, or famine, or nakedness, or peril, or sword?'*

Nothing could ever separate us from the love Christ has for us, but I do know one thing that has separated Him from our love. It is simply this thing we call our money. If we give it over to Christ (again, I don't mean giving all of it physically to Kingdom work) with the understanding that it is His to do with as He wills, while directing us, then He might just ask us to do some things that we might not have a desire to do. It might not be a part of *our* heart's treasures.

I have been amazed over the past two years with some of the books and articles I've read. Not necessarily bad or good writing or even writing on economics or books on faith—these are writings that have been published since we have been in the midst of this financial crisis. All kinds of people want to capitalize on it. Someone told me, "Dan, I love some of the things that you have written. We need people like you to continue to write about the economy—people who understand the goings on of politics and legislation and how it affects our world from an economic standpoint." This tells me that the books these people are writing are not very clear, and the reason they're not clear is because they're not full of truth. Truth is very simple, and clear. A child can understand the gospel.

One of the greatest compliments I received along those lines was from someone who said, "When you write it or say it, we understand it—and we need you to do more of it. Allow the theologians to write about our faith." I am astounded as I see so many people wanting to capitalize on the area of finance. Anything about finances, end-times, or material like that is admittedly an entertaining read and an easy sell. And it's perplexing how many theologians are now writing about finance, from an end-times perspective. So since many theologians are now writing about the economy, I feel more comfortable writing about things of faith.

I am sad to say that I cannot begin to tell you how many quotes I have read by some wonderful teachers of God's Word (some of my favorites), who have made some economic statements that are not even close to being accurate. Having said that, I am sure my hermeneutics (or my interpretations of particular verses) can sometimes be a stretch, and *maybe* my interpretation may not be as theologically eloquent as some of the great preachers and teachers. I do however, know this, we cannot separate finance and faith.

I know that those theology majors (as I also happen to be) make financial statements because there is a necessity to bring financial discussion back to the arena of faith and into God's Word. We cannot go on any longer separating our finances; separating what we consider is uncomfortable to take before God. If we are going to give our lives to Christ, then we need to give Him *everything* in our lives. We need to make the greatest book on economics—the Bible—a part of our family economics.

One of the people to whom I absolutely love to listen, is David Barton of WallBuilders.[1] Several years ago, as part of a small group of national religious broadcasters, David gave a private tour of the Capitol Building in Washington, D.C. This was after-hours and he had the freedom to take us into places that official tours might not normally go, which was really a treat. The greatest thing about David Barton is his unique ability to keep the Word of God central to every aspect of our Republic, every aspect of the Constitution and the laws that are being passed, even today.

---

1 www.WallBuilders.com

If our legislators would have stayed on course and continued to follow the moral compass—the incredible book of ethics that the Bible is—we would not be in the national financial mess we are in today. For this reason, I continue to write in such a way as to weave the economic structure of our society and family in with the mandates and duties that are pointed out to us in the Word of God. We cannot forget the foundational piece of all of our financial transactions. We cannot forget the foundational piece of being a good financial steward, which is to be good stewards of the gospel of Jesus Christ, as set forth in the Word of God!

I love Paul's attitude when he wrote the book of Colossians. Paul was in a very uncomfortable position, likely in a Roman prison, when he wrote that letter to the Colossians. In chapter one, starting in verse 24-25, he says,

> *'24 I now rejoice in my sufferings for you, and fill up in my flesh what is lacking in the afflictions of Christ, for the sake of His body, which is the church, 25 of which I became a minister according to the stewardship from God which was given to me for you, to fulfill the word of God,'*

We may be struggling, and we may have situations in our financial life that we just can't seem to give over to Christ. But we too, if we know the Lord, are very similar to Paul. Although we may struggle and suffer and have trials and heartaches, we too—first and foremost—are stewards as ministers of God. I'm certain that many of you have never thought of yourself as a minister of God or a steward of the gospel, but you are. If only our legislators and those in Washington would believe that they have an obligation to be a good steward of what the people of their districts have entrusted to them—to be a good steward of the Constitution under all circumstances, with the principles found in the Bible as their guide, we'd be on a much better national path. But you can insure your family remains on the right path, and when enough of us are doing this, it will affect these leaders, and ultimately the entire nation.

Paul held on to that glorious job which he was given to get him through some very difficult times. We often, instead of holding on to our work for the sake of God, seem to let that part of it go when it comes to our suffering from a financial perspective. God not only *wants* us to give it over to Him, He expects us to do so. He wants us to expect that *He* will take care of our struggles. We should be committed to God in all things—not all things *except* our finances. All means all. We need to realize how great a Treasure He is, and trust Him to take care of all our needs.

Ultimately, it comes down to our focus. Do we wake up in a panic over our finances? Do we shake God and tell Him to wake up because surely we will perish (like the disciples in the boat)? Do we shake the Lord and say, "What is going on? Please help us." I think many of us try to do that when we have reached a point where we are finally willing to give those circumstances over to God. I know from a financial perspective, this can sometimes be a good thing for the non-believer. *I was one of them.* I have been in some incredibly harsh circumstances throughout my life in a number of areas. None of those things could ever convince me to rely on God. None of those circumstances could ever convince me that I needed the saving grace of Jesus Christ as my personal Lord and Savior. No one could ever begin to convince me (though many had tried) that if I came to Christ, my life could change. But one thing finally did get a hold of me. It was that moment when I realized that everything I had worked so hard for was gone. That was when I realized that although I thought I could do anything, I could *not* get myself out of the circumstances that I was in.

It took losing huge sums of money, the one thing that I worshipped, for me to fall apart, before I would ever come to the knowledge of God. Not even a threat on my life would have turned me to God, but a threat to my financial well-being was the one thing that was going to do that. In fact, God had used my worship of money and the financial turmoil that I was in to soften my heart and call me to Him. He'll quickly pinpoint what is left in your heart that you're not willing to give up to find all of Him.

I have often said how important radio is to me. My ministry has been on the radio for fourteen years, and I am extremely grateful for that opportunity. Christian radio, however, is not just a means by which I get to communicate to people and help them with their financial circumstances. It holds a special place for *me*. I was one of those people, as a result of Charles Stanley's radio ministry, who pulled over on the side of the road and gave my life to Christ. I remember how, for five years, my wife thought I had gone nuts as I poured through Scripture, completed my Masters Degree in Theology, and listened to Christian radio. I am not much of a sleeper and I am usually up very early in the morning. I had a waterproof transistor radio so that every morning, at about 4 or 4:30 a.m. (I don't remember the exact time since it was well over twenty-five years ago.), I would get into the shower and listen to J. Vernon McGee.

I remember my wife said so many times, "How can you listen to that man with that annoying voice?" But, I didn't know any other believers, so the radio not only led me to the Lord, but it also discipled me for a good many years. Maybe that's part of the reason I am so committed to American Family Radio. Christian radio plays an important part in my life and I am privileged to be a part of it. Christian radio was also instrumental in my wife coming to the Lord. One day, because of something I heard Dennis Rainey say on the radio, I turned my car around and drove two hours back home. I called my wife and asked her to meet me. We sat and talked about my faith for three hours and the following weekend we went to a marriage conference where my wife accepted Christ. This was all because of radio ministries. It took hours of listening to Charles Stanley's radio ministry to get me to the point where I realized that Jesus was that great Treasure. The Pearl of great price. When I did, I never looked back, and never regretted a single day following that decision.

I say all of this to share with you that I *do* know a thing or two about the desire to hang on to those things that have to do with our finances. I know that there are many of you who are reading this, who find it impossible to not hang onto your money. You feel like you simply can't give that control over to Christ. Perhaps you have a fear of what He might tell you to do with it. Maybe you have convinced yourself that you don't want to "bother" Him with that. Believe me, He wants to be bothered with it. Perhaps some of you don't want the conviction that might come from God as you pray and give that portion of your life over to Him. But consider that what we have done is missed out on the opportunity to know what God can do with our money and to our heart when we give it over to Him.

Theologians who write about economics and economists who write about theology have one thing very much in common; both understand that one cannot be separated from the other. No more than one can separate the legislative process of the United States of America from a knowledge of the Bible. I have often heard David Barton speak of how SAT scores in this country have been on a continual downward spiral since 1962, when we took God out of the classroom. Yet, SAT scores among homeschoolers and the grades of private Christian schools have continued to climb.

This is because all of the learning which comes to homeschoolers and those in the private Christian schools is based upon the foundation of the Bible. All the knowledge in the world is worthless if we do not have what is contained in God's Word. Yet, we want to separate the knowledge, commitment, and conviction we have in God's Word from the very thing which *He* can *multiply* to give us rest. Our money. We must give it all to Jesus, and I don't mean that in a physical way, but a place in our hearts where we can say, "Take control of our finances, Lord, and help us make good decisions and continue to provide for our needs—not our wants—but our needs. You are the great Treasure, Lord, and we put you above everything else."

If you are struggling through some financial heartaches, take a moment and think about whether you truly gave them over to Christ and then *stepped away*. This is the key. Be sure you are not continuing to meddle in what the Lord is doing or continuing to check on Him to "make sure" that it is going the way *you* would like it to go. Just trust Him. Give Him control. Have you truly given it over to Him and stepped away from it? We must give all things to Christ, and put Him first. Our fear of losing money, or of the lack of money will change as our perspective changes and as the desire of our heart changes.

# Chapter Five

# **What Shall I Do?**

There are certainly many ways by which we can change our attitude toward our finances. We can change the way we think about our debt, our lack of money, or perhaps our inability to make ends meet. If you are of the mindset that under your circumstances "How could we possibly give anything to our church or to the Lord's work?" you might need a change in the way you think about your money. Let's take another look at Jesus's parable of the rich man in the book of Luke:

> *'16 Then He spoke a parable to them, saying:*
> *"The ground of a certain rich man yielded*
> *plentifully. 17 And he thought within himself,*

*saying, 'What shall I do, since I have no room to store my crops?' 18 So he said, 'I will do this: I will pull down my barns and build greater, and there I will store all my crops and my goods. 19 And I will say to my soul, "Soul, you have many goods laid up for many years; take your ease; eat, drink, and be merry."'* **Luke 12:16-19**

This man was obviously a very well-to-do farmer. Notice how he starts out with "What shall I do?" His question of "What should I do?" came as a result of having a lot more than he needed or a lot more than, I assume, he even anticipated. Notice also in this parable, that the rich man uses the word "I" or "my" eleven times. Certainly this was an individual who was focused on himself. Understand that when we start to compartmentalize our finances away from God, we have no choice but to internalize and focus all of our financial considerations on ourselves. If you read on to verse 20, God called this man a fool, because he was laying up treasures on earth, and for what? That night he died.

Sadly for this man, the question here of "What should I do?" is a very simple one to answer. We should do as *Scripture* tells us to, yet we seem to compartmentalize *Scripture as well* when it comes to our finances. Some would compartmentalize Scripture to use it falsely to preach a *Prosperity Gospel* which says that if you give it all to Jesus (*or in reality to "my" church or "my" ministry*), you will be blessed. Some use it to justify the internalizing of their riches, like the rich man Jesus spoke about. These *motives* are incorrect.

I'll mention here that without a sound, underlying belief that Scripture is the inspired Word of God, you will find it very difficult to be obedient to God in the areas that are most challenging—such as your money. Look at what the apostle Paul says:

> '*All Scripture is given by inspiration of God, and is profitable for doctrine, for reproof, for correction, for instruction in righteousness,*'
> **2 Timothy 3:16**

I'll go so far as to say that many, many Christians do not have a deep understanding that the Bible is the absolute, infallible Word of God. Many profess as much but when it comes to actually putting something into practice, or being obedient we sort of try to twist the meaning, or some even (heretically) go so far as to say the Bible doesn't actually mean what it says, and it's all open for interpretation. The truth is that the Word of God is the foundation for all we believe. Scientifically, it is the most consistent document in history.

When we understand that God means what He says, and His written Word is to be trusted, and it's warnings to be taken seriously, we are at a starting point for practical faith. This is the beginning of the answer to "What shall I do?" The answer can only come from the Word of God, the Bible. This is why there are so many attacks in America today on having the Bible as a public representation of our founding faith. If Satan can get people to doubt the trustworthiness of the Bible, he removes the bedrock on which the power of God rests for those who doubt. But we *can* trust the Bible, and claim all of God's promises when we are obedient.

What we need to do is to understand and believe God's promises throughout Scripture, whether it is speaking to good behavior or bad. In Proverbs 11:28, it says, *'He who trusts in his riches will fall, But the righteous will flourish like foliage.'* I think it is interesting that God (through King Solomon) uses the words "will fall." He does not say "*might* fall," "*could* fall," "*should* fall," or "*will likely* fall." He says "will fall." Just above that, in verse 25, He says *"The generous soul will be made rich, And he who waters will also be watered himself."* In verse 26, it says *"The people will curse him who withholds grain."*

Certainly God is reminding us that we are to be generous and give always. First of all, we should rely on the promises of God which say He will take care of our struggles *or* our riches, as He will speak to our hearts in a way that will help us deal with them. He will not, by the way, leave us to our own resources *if* we are asking and giving it over to Him. *"The generous soul will be made rich,"* He says. I don't believe that this necessarily always means *earthly* riches or material possessions, but I am perfectly okay with taking my blessings in Heaven for the faithfulness of my giving here on earth. But whether God wishes to bless me here on earth because He knows He can trust me as a channel of blessing to others, or if my reward is in Heaven, the point is that God prefers us to be generous.

So then in the parable of the rich man, when he asked the question of himself, "What shall I do?" his internal dialogue should have gone as follows: *"I have far more than I need and since God is the One who has blessed me so abundantly, that abundance is therefore His. I should do with it what would be pleasing to Him."* Instead, the rich man made a conscious choice toward greed. It is true that this choice was driven by fear, and a need for security, but that is no excuse. God knows we can do better. The choice becomes dangerous when we consciously ignore the fact that God has provided the blessing, and try to take credit as though we had anything to do with the increase. If we are to take credit for anything, let it be in that we are obedient to God.

Make no mistake—we all have a responsibility for the choices we have made. Some of us are suffering for choices which we made before we knew the Lord. Others may be suffering in *spite* of the fact that they have come to the Lord, because they *continue* to make poor choices, contrary to what the Word instructs. I promise you because I have practiced it, and it is tried and true—the best thing you can do for your future is begin to be obedient to God in what you know He is telling you to do.

What we should do is recognize that there *are* consequences for our choices, and we should ask God for wisdom and rely on Him to give us that wisdom. Understand that the "little or a lot" that He has given us is not really ours, but that we have a stewardship responsibility for it. What we need to do is to visit Scripture often and pray often, and you'll be amazed at how He will show you where and how you can give to the Lord what is rightfully His.

I have frequently said that I have yet to meet anyone who has been faithful in their giving that has financial burdens or problems. I have sat with countless missionaries who have spent thirty or forty years on the mission field, serving the Lord and got paid practically nothing, yet are still trying to figure out how they managed to accumulate so much money for the balance of their days on earth. I have seen firsthand the power of God when we give all of our life's possessions to Him. What we should do is pray to have a heart and an attitude of a generous servant of God. We may not be able to give as our heart would desire, but the desire in our heart should be strong and intentional. Then watch how the Lord will bless us—maybe not always materially but always with his abundant grace and wisdom. And what could be better than that?

# Chapter Six

# The Law of Sowing and Reaping

The parable of the sower is such an important one that it is found in three of the four gospels, and Jesus implies that it is the key to understanding all other parables. Look at what He says to His disciples in Mark 4:

> 'And He said to them, "Do you not understand this parable? How then will you understand all the parables?' **Mark 4:13**

Why is this parable so important? I'll give you a hint—it concerns the heart, and the heart is cultivating ground for fear or faith. Take a look at the parable and I'll expound on it.

> '3 "*Listen! Behold, a sower went out to sow. 4 And it happened, as he sowed, that some seed fell by the wayside; and the birds of the air[a] came and devoured it. 5 Some fell on stony ground, where it did not have much earth; and immediately it sprang up because it had no depth of earth. 6 But when the sun was up it was scorched, and because it had no root it withered away. 7 And some seed fell among thorns; and the thorns grew up and choked it, and it yielded no crop. 8 But other seed fell on good ground and yielded a crop that sprang up, increased and produced: some thirtyfold, some sixty, and some a hundred."* '**Mark 4:3-8**

In this parable, Jesus goes on to explain that the ground He is talking about here is the human heart (or spirit). If you read closely you will see yourself somewhere in one of these examples. Every single person is covered here. You know the person who is instantly skeptical, and even though the truth is represented clearly and plainly, they will always find a reason to dismiss it, simply because they will have to change if they receive it. (Satan blinds them to how profitable that change would be to them.)

The next example is someone who is, in modern terms, "flaky." When they first hear the truth, they're all gung-ho, and then lose steam and burn out, and eventually avoid it at all cost. They have no root, or integrity. Their word is not their bond. Sadly, many people in America live in this state. They have been to church, and think they have seen it and done it already. They have no idea that anything worth something takes consistent effort for a period of time, before you see something grow.

Next, is another type of people. Those are the ones who would do really well otherwise, but tend to look at the "waves" like the apostle Peter did when he walked on the water with Jesus. These are people who have some integrity, and mean well but they allow life's cares and burdens to overshadow their trust in God. In the context of finances and giving, this example is very relevant.

Lastly, we see those who hear and accept the Word. That word "hear" means "understand." Notice there is a three-part process there; first they hear and understand the Word. Then they accept it—that is they make it their own, make it a part of their life—they *apply* it. Then they produce a good crop. In fact, God does the last part. How fruitful you are, how much crop you produce, depends on how much you apply the Word and trust God and He gives the increase!

These verses are so important. I open every radio program with a recorded clip of Billy Graham saying, "The Bible says be not deceived, whatsoever a man soweth, that he shall also reap." I guess it is my hope that I drive that message home. In the context of this book, I wanted to use this illustration at this point to highlight the fact that as you read, *now* is the time to decide if you're going to accept this word. Accepting it means applying it. You can read all the books in the world, but only the ones you allow to be applied in your life will make a difference—for good or bad. Even as I sit here doing a bit of a rewrite on this chapter, I am writing from a pew in the chapel at the Billy Graham Training Center in North Carolina. My wife and I are here for the weekend allowing some cultivation to take place in our own hearts. Your heart is the area where everything happens, and Jesus used farming imagery for a reason. Your heart grows whatever is cultivated in it.

Now that we understand the parable of the sower, let's take a look at the law of sowing and reaping.

> *'7 Do not be deceived, God is not mocked;*
> *for whatever a man sows, that he will also*
> *reap. 8 For he who sows to his flesh will of*

*the flesh reap corruption, but he who sows to the Spirit will of the Spirit reap everlasting life. 9 And let us not grow weary while doing good, for in due season we shall reap if we do not lose heart. 10 Therefore, as we have opportunity, let us do good to all, especially to those who are of the household of faith.'*
**Galatians 6:7-10**

That is powerful. The apostle Paul says that believing we will reap what we didn't sow, or believing we will not reap what we have sown, is like mocking God. There is good news in this law, though. Everything good you do for the Kingdom will come back to you. There are so many Scriptures that show that an entire book could be compiled just of those Scriptures. Read the book of Proverbs and you'll find so many of these promises in there, it will cast out any doubt that giving to Kingdom work, and providing for the needy (both financially and spiritually) will bring great blessing into your life.

Notice that Paul says *"for in due season we shall reap if we do not lose heart."* Now tie this in with the parable of the sower—*"for in due season."* Remember the second example? The flaky ones? They gave up before their season came due! In fact, the second and third examples both give up as well, for various reasons. The key is sticking with your giving, until you begin to see changes in your church, changes in your family, and changes in your own life.

Now the question I know that some of you again will have is, "Are you talking about a prosperity gospel? Are you saying that the more we give, if we just hang on, God will make us rich?" No, what I'm saying is that when you allow your heart to be pliable and used by God, there is no limit to what He can do with you and through you. But you have to keep your heart humble, and obedient to God's word, and stick with it and in *due time* He will bring about change. If you can't give control of your money to God, how are you going to give control of anything to Him, since money represents your life effort?

But be aware that blessings don't always come in the form of money. God could change the heart of that family member you've been praying for. He could cause your car to hold out for another year. He could heal you of disease, saving thousands in medical bills. He could give you the inspiration for an idea that will bring you and the Kingdom millions of dollars. The point is that if you have a fear of money, your heart is not accessible to God. If your heart is not accessible to God, there is only so much He can do to bless you, and continue the work of His kingdom *through you.*

In the same way, I will say here that money is not the only way you can sow into the Kingdom. You can volunteer your time, you can witness to people you meet, and you can donate items you don't need any longer. All of these things are considered sowing righteousness. That becomes fairly obvious when viewed in the light of what we discussed about money simply being symbolic of our daily effort. We don't get paid for volunteering at our church, but it is guaranteed there is great value in that service. You don't get paid when you donate clothes or a car to a ministry, but you are guaranteed that is of great value.

The beauty of the matter is this; sowing and reaping is a spiritual *law*. If you give to the work of the Kingdom (with the right heart), you're sowing spiritually, and God promises you will reap life. This means eternal life, but it also means the life that is bundled with salvation—peace, joy, love and yes, I believe that if your priorities are right, God will be able to bless you financially and give you wisdom to make the right choices that will lead to having all your needs met. This is all true IF you don't give up before your harvest. You have to make a decision to give up that fear of money, grow your faith, and become a giver to Kingdom work, and then do it consistently and watch and expect God to bring changes into your life where you need it most. It is a spiritual law. It *must* happen.

I love what the prophet Hosea said, centuries before Christ was born:

> *'Sow for yourselves righteousness; Reap in mercy; Break up your fallow ground, For it is time to seek the LORD, till He comes and rains righteousness on you.'* **Hosea 10:12**

Do you see here, long before Jesus was born, God is speaking through the prophet Hosea saying your heart is the unplowed ground. God is urging us to break it up, and seek Him until He comes and showers His righteousness on us. God tells us to sow righteousness, and reap the fruit of God's unfailing love—which is His complete provision. But we have to break up our unplowed hearts. If we have a fear of giving God control of our lives, or a fear of money, we have stony, hard hearts—and that is not God's best for us. He is so loving He continues to bless us any way He can, but He has much, much more for us. You see, it's in God's interest to bless you so you can bless others. He's in the business of multiplication. So break up your stony heart today, and give God control of it, and watch what He does with your life when you're completely surrendered to him.

# Chapter Seven

# To One Who Has Been Entrusted With Much

I believe one of the problems many Christians face is not knowing our authority and power on earth. This in turn is tied to not knowing our identity. We've been told our identity is found in Christ, but when we truly study and understand this, it is one of the most powerful revelations a believer will have.

> '3 Blessed be the God and Father of our Lord Jesus Christ, who has blessed us with every spiritual blessing in the heavenly places in Christ, 4 just as He chose us in Him before

*the foundation of the world, that we should be holy and without blame before Him in love, 5 having predestined us to adoption as sons by Jesus Christ to Himself, according to the good pleasure of His will, 6 to the praise of the glory of His grace, by which He made us accepted in the Beloved. 7 In Him we have redemption through His blood, the forgiveness of sins, according to the riches of His grace 8 which He made to abound toward us in all wisdom and prudence,'*
**Ephesians 1:3-8**

In the Scripture above, Paul is writing to the believers in Ephesus, explaining the vastness of what is covered in salvation. Many of us stop at just being saved from eternal destruction, but it is so much more than that. Paul says here that God has blessed us with *"every spiritual blessing in the heavenly places in Christ."* This means that every good and necessary gift has already been "awarded" to us, through Jesus Christ. Notice I said awarded—you have a legal right to all you need, but Satan will try to challenge you and rob you of appropriating these blessings. If you are unaware of your identity this becomes much easier for him.

Remember that God the Father, Jesus, and the Holy Spirit are royalty. You don't get higher royalty than Godhood. We have been adopted into this royal family through the payment of Jesus Christ. This means that while you are fretting over whether you are going to be able to make ends meet, you are in fact, royalty, in full ownership of all of Christ's blessings. Now, to reiterate, the goal on earth is to win souls. There is nothing more valuable here than a soul. That is our goal, so righteous desires are to have enough to take care of our family, and then begin supporting the work of the Kingdom. This is mature wisdom. Look at what the book of Proverbs says:

> *'The fruit of the righteous is a tree of life,*
> *And he who wins souls is wise.'*
> **Proverbs 11:30**

The original Hebrew translation says something more like "He that is wise, wins souls." We are so much more empowered for the work of the Kingdom, when we realize just how magnificent that Kingdom is. Part of coming to that realization is understanding we are royalty in that magnificent Kingdom and studying our identity in Christ. I highly recommend you do a quick internet search for "identity in Christ Scriptures" and read through some Scriptures that address who you are in Christ. Only when you truly start walking in that knowledge, and perspective, can you begin to affect others' lives in ways you would never have dreamed possible. Without this knowledge, it is very easy to keep falling back into an area of complacency and fear. This will always affect your support of the Kingdom's work.

Now I want to tell you a secret that will help you in every area of your life, and walk with Christ. It is a secret that when you truly understand, and apply to your daily life, will turn your stagnant efforts into a pouring flood of blessing. It is found in the Scripture below:

> *'The fear of the LORD is the beginning of wisdom, And the knowledge of the Holy One is understanding.'* **Proverbs 9:10**

That word *fear* means a holy reverence, as well as a healthy fear of the sovereign God of eternity. It has connotations of humble respect for the highest ranking military commander, and ultimately can be practiced as humility. Humility is the key to receiving from God. Take a look at the next Scripture:

> *'But He gives more grace. Therefore He says: "God resists the proud, But gives grace to the humble.'* **James 4:6**

We are royalty, but remember when Jesus washed the disciples' feet and also told them that the highest leader is a servant to all? God favors humility. When we submit our will and our personal plan for our lives to His will and plan, it greatly pleases Him, and He will show you special favor. Believe me, God can do infinitely more with your life than you could ever hope to. And He can do it quickly if He wants to. In fact, to the degree you can submit to His will, is the degree He can use you. The fear of the Lord—not an unhealthy fear, but humility and reverence—will bring favor to your life and as you submit to His will in the areas in which He is speaking to your heart, He will begin to bless you, and bless you in many and various ways. Your children will be obedient. Your spouse will be more content. Your boss will recognize your good work. You will make connections that will bring about a greater increase in your life. Most of all, you will become a channel of blessing. Once God is given control of your life, He can use you to bless others. Do you think the conduit won't receive blessings while it is being used? Of course not. A law in Deuteronomy 25:4 says, *'"You shall not muzzle an ox while it treads out the grain.'* This simply means a worker is allowed to eat of the fruit of his or her labor. That means God will bless you, while He is using you to bless others! But you have to allow Him to.

I want to change tone for a minute, and talk about the flip side of this wonderful coin. I'm sure many of you have heard the phrase "Ignorance is no defense." What this means in legal terms, is that being ignorant of a law does not excuse you from breaking it. God's Kingdom works in this same way. In fact, because believers have the Holy Spirit within us speaking to our conscience, we cannot really claim ignorance. We almost always know better. In light of all that God has given us through Christ, surely we should desire that the lost experience this, too? Our unsaved loved ones? Our unsaved neighbors? Colleagues? Friends?

God has blessed us and is very patient with us, but when we become stuck on something as trivial as money (it really is in the larger scheme of human souls), God has to draw the line somewhere. Disobedience always has a cost, and it's very high. You see, this is why it is so important for us to "hit the ground running" when we first accept Christ. There is that joy, and relief of being saved from our sin and eternal destruction, that carries momentum. For those of you who were just "born into" a Christian family, and you've never experienced this joy, you need to read your Bible very closely, and study exactly what you were born into! It is anything but dull.

We are to be excited about the gospel, and how it has the power to change lives all around us. But this has to become a revelation to us first. If it isn't then you have not fully surrendered your life to God. Surrendering your life to

God means being obedient when Jesus told us to pray. Paul commands the same thing in 1 Thessalonians 5:17. We are to study the Bible because the Bible is the Word of God, and is literally the written person of Christ (the Logos in the Greek.) You are to know God because your life will become enriched, and you will be equipped to enrich others in the same way.

If ignorance is no defense, then surely complacency is unjustifiable. We've scratched the surface in this chapter, but when you understand all you have been given when you accept Christ as your Lord and Savior, you will see that a great responsibility comes with this gift. Faithfulness is a word that means more than just marital fidelity. It means faithfulness in what you know God has called you to do. He meets you wherever you are, and if it means simply going to church consistently then start there, and grow. If it means committing to give 10 percent to your church, come hell or high-water, then start there, and grow. If it means going into full-time ministry, then you had better seriously seek God and be obedient to whatever He reveals to you. I believe an excellent starting place for many Christians is supporting the work of ministry and their church with their finances. Giving invests you in the Kingdom. It is almost impossible to give absent-mindedly to someone. You wouldn't give just *anyone* your money would you? So giving immediately gets you involved in the Kingdom work, if for nothing else than researching, and making sure the recipient is legitimate (you should always do this by the way).

God is a loving Father and compassionate Lord, but He is also a just judge. You have been given so much in salvation, that claiming ignorance of God's will for you to grow in your walk with Him, and your support of Kingdom work, is absolutely no defense. He expects you to bear fruit, just as we read in the chapter which explains your heart is like a garden. Look at what Jesus says in the gospel of Luke:

> *'42 And the Lord said, "Who then is that faithful and wise steward, whom his master will make ruler over his household, to give them their portion of food in due season? 43 Blessed is that servant whom his master will find so doing when he comes. 44 Truly, I say to you that he will make him ruler over all that he has. 45 But if that servant says in his heart, 'My master is delaying his coming,' and begins to beat the male and female servants, and to eat and drink and be drunk, 46 the master of that servant will come on a day when he is not looking for him, and at an hour when he is not aware, and will cut him in two and appoint him his portion with the unbelievers. 47 And that servant who knew his master's will, and did not prepare*

*himself or do according to his will, shall be
beaten with many stripes. 48 But he who did
not know, yet committed things deserving
of stripes, shall be beaten with few. For
everyone to whom much is given, from him
much will be required; and to whom much
has been committed, of him they will ask the
more.'* **Luke 12:42-48**

This is one of those Scriptures that we almost prefer to
not read, since it carries such a heavy responsibility with
it. Jesus makes it perfectly clear that God expects us to be
faithful, work hard, and be found doing Kingdom work when
Jesus returns. Notice in this parable, there are three types of
disobedient servants.

The first type is a believer who simply gets impatient.
He says, *'My master is delaying his coming.'* He begins to
basically act like the world, and live as an unsaved person.
The master arrives on a day when the servant doesn't expect
(judgment always arrives at a time we don't expect) and the
servant is essentially cast out, and regarded as an unbeliever.
This is a very, scary example, and I'm sure you understand
the connotations.

The next example of a disobedient servant is one who
knows the will of God, but either is complacent (does not

get ready) or does not do what the master expects (outright disobedience). This servant keeps their place in the house but is punished severely, and probably loses a significant amount of rank or title.

The final example is a servant who seemingly doesn't know better, but is still complacent, is still punished. This is because these servants have been living in the master's house, with great privilege. Ignorance is not a defense.

I'm sure you can see the parallels to Christian life. We as believers are to work as wise stewards of the Kingdom of God. Every believer has a very unique, special purpose to their life, and God has called you to fulfill yours. God expects us to keep growing, and to bear fruit in our Christian walk. He requires us to submit to His will, and to seek and get to know Him, personally. He loves us greatly, but can only extend grace so far. If we are insistent on being either blatantly disobedient and living like the unsaved, or being complacent, He has to discipline us. This is because we have been given so much, at such a high price (in fact, the blood of Christ is priceless,) it is a slap in God's face to regard this salvation as common, and revert to pursuing our own agenda above God's.

Something amazing happens however, when we submit our will to God's, and live faithfully. We are increasingly freed from all of our fears, including one of the most dominant—the fear of money! When we start living as righteous royalty, operating as God's stewards on this earth, we understand that we are simply a conduit of His blessing, and His will. All we have, all we are, is God's. He gave it to us in the first place, just like He gave the increase to the rich man who received a great crop. When we submit all we are to Him, we are trading fear for faith, and faith is what really moves God!

> *'But without faith it is impossible to please Him, for he who comes to God must believe that He is, and that He is a rewarder of those who diligently seek Him.'* **Hebrews 11:6**

I urge you to trade fear for faith today. Repent of complacency and disobedience, and commit your heart to walking faithfully with God. Begin praying every day, and studying your Bible, to understand God's will for your life. Start loving and helping anyone who needs it, and you'll see God begin to bring divine favor into your life. And when God's favor begins to flow in your life, you will truly understand how God is a God of multiplication! In fact, I explain this fascinating mystery in the next chapter.

# Chapter Eight

# The Paradigm of Multiplication

I've spoken about sowing and reaping as a metaphor for the heart, but God also has a very literal meaning for sowing and reaping. In many Scriptures, the Bible talks about sowing and reaping in the plain and simple context of giving and receiving. In large part, these Scriptures speak directly to finances.

I really like a Scripture the apostle Paul writes in 2 Corinthians. In fact, I believe hidden in these verses is a key to God's paradigm of multiplication. Take a look:

> *'6 But this I say: He who sows sparingly*
> *will also reap sparingly, and he who sows*

*bountifully will also reap bountifully. 7 So let each one give as he purposes in his heart, not grudgingly or of necessity; for God loves a cheerful giver. 8 And God is able to make all grace abound toward you, that you, always having all sufficiency in all things, may have an abundance for every good work. 9 As it is written:*

> *"He has dispersed abroad,*
> *He has given to the poor;*
> *His righteousness endures forever."*

*10 Now may He who supplies seed to the sower, and bread for food, supply and multiply the seed you have sown and increase the fruits of your righteousness, 11 while you are enriched in everything for all liberality, which causes thanksgiving through us to God.'* **2 Corinthians 9:6-11**

I would like to break down this Scripture piece by piece, and examine exactly what Paul is saying here. First he says, *'He who sows sparingly will also reap sparingly, and he who sows bountifully will also reap bountifully.'* Many of God's laws are found in nature too, and Jesus often referred to nature metaphors. This makes sense because God used a specific design for Creation, and it wouldn't make sense for Him to use arbitrary laws to base His creation upon. No, He used His spiritual laws as a foundation. This is why Jesus often used this sort of parable. It is easy for us to relate to and understand.

When Paul says whoever sows sparingly will reap sparingly, it only makes sense, right? If you listen to some angry Christians you have to wonder what they're thinking. They'll say, "Why doesn't God do this for me," or "Why did He allow that to happen?" All the while you know the situation; they're not even putting in the effort needed to get the thing started, or something bad happened to them because they lived recklessly and without wisdom for years, and it finally caught up with them. No, what you sow, you reap. It's a natural law. It's a spiritual law. You don't sow ten seeds and twenty tomato plants spring up? No, you'll be blessed if all ten of them spring up! But we as Christians tend to think God is a magic fairy Godfather or something who will just wave a wand when we give him ten seconds flat, twice a day in requests. I'll say it in plain, old American English. It ain't gonna happen!

Likewise, if we sow to the Kingdom of God sparingly, we will reap sparingly. And if we sow generously, we will reap generously. This little piece of wisdom could change your life. Okay. I hope you get the point.

Next Paul says, *'So let each one give as he purposes in his heart, not grudgingly or of necessity.'* I love this sentence because again, it addresses the heart response to giving. Notice he says *each* of you should give as you have decided in your *heart*. First, the *each* means it is an individual decision. Yes, a married couple should and must discuss their marital Kingdom giving, but what I believe Paul is saying here is you should individually seek the Lord as to what, and how much you should give. Pray and ask the Holy Spirit what you should give and He'll lead you. You'll have a peace about what He tells you to give, if you take the time to hear His voice. I promise you.

Next, notice that he says, *'as he purposes in his heart.'* This means once you have decided, remain firm and give what you have decided. Don't be double-minded. The apostle James speaks about being double-minded. He says a double-minded person should expect nothing of the Lord (James 1:7-8.) It is the equivalent of sowing seeds in the ground and ripping them out after a day or two.

The second part of the last sentence is *'not grudgingly or of necessity; for God loves a cheerful giver.'* Paul is saying decide in your heart what to give, and be happy about it. Never, ever give reluctantly nor under compulsion. God cannot bless this attitude. It is actually better for you not to give in this mindset. It shows that you have neither prepared your heart before God, nor have you carefully considered where to give. Now, just as your heart needs to be good ground, I believe you should also carefully consider where God would want you to sow your seed. Some ministries are better ground than others. In fact, if any ministry is manipulative in attempting to get you to give, they are probably not good ground. The giveaway is whether or not they can base their teachings in Scripture. Give wisely and you'll have peace. Give as the Holy Spirit leads you. You have to spend a little time asking Him though.

Next, Paul says, *'And God is able to make all grace abound toward you, that you, always having all sufficiency in all things, may have an abundance for every good work.'* I love this part of the Scripture because it completely captures the reason we give. God wants to bless you abundantly so that in **all** things, at **all** times, having **all** that you need, you will have an abundance for every good work! Did you get that God wants you to be completely blessed? Yes, that's the reason Paul used three "alls" right there. God wants you blessed ALL the time in everything you need, so that you can have abundance or for every good work. According to Dictionary.com's definition "abundance" means *"an extremely plentiful or oversufficient quantity or supply an extremely plentiful or oversufficient quantity or supply."* Yes, God wants you blessed. Why? So that you can abound in every good work. God wants you to be a conduit! He wants you to be a channel, so that others can be blessed in all things, at all times, having all they need, so that God's

Kingdom can grow, and grow, and grow! This is how God works! He requires fruit from a single seed, and this is how He accomplishes it. He blesses first, so we can bless others and it becomes a fascinating case study in multiplication. Good works are the focus, and He wants you to abound in every good work! Oh, please note, He gives for our needs not our wants. So many people over the years have said to me, "God has not ever blessed me abundantly." What they mean to say is, "forget my needs I was hoping for riches."

I really like verse 9 too: *'As it is written: "He has dispersed abroad, He has given to the poor; His righteousness endures forever."'* This Scripture is originally found in Psalm 112:9, and speaks again of eternal rewards to giving, way back then in King David's time. If it was true then, your good works have eternal consequences now, too. The love you show a family in need, by perhaps buying them groceries, demonstrates the love of Christ where words are feeble. When they turn to God because of your kindness, God attributes their salvation to you! And God will make sure your storehouse is always full because He knows you are going to abound in every good work with what He gives you!

This is what Paul is getting at in the next verse where he says, *'Now may He who supplies seed to the sower, and bread for food, supply and multiply the seed you have sown and increase the fruits of your righteousness.'* Notice that God supplies seed to the sower (you) AND He supplies bread for food. It's easy to overlook the significance of what is being said here, but Paul is actually saying God differentiates between two types of income you receive. One is seed. One is bread. One you are supposed to eat. One you are supposed to give. The good news is that God is supplying both! You don't have to worry about it. All you have to do is make sure you aren't eating your seed. And that's easy to do. Consider the Old Testament example of manna, when the Israelites were in the wilderness (Exod. 16.) God told Moses He would rain down heavenly bread, called manna, to feed the people. The Israelites were to gather up enough for just that day. If they gathered up any more, it would be rotten by the next morning. Every day God rained down more manna. On the sixth day, they were to gather enough for two days, so they wouldn't have to collect on the Sabbath. This demonstrates that the manna would stay fresh for two days if God wanted it to. It was an amazing miracle.

What does this have to do with seed and bread? Easy. Just "eat" enough for what you need, and God will provide more for tomorrow. Work hard but no need to overwork to become rich. Trust God and He will provide for every good work, and He will provide "bread" for your needs. He knows what your heart's desires are. If you want your children to go to a good college, raise them in the ways of the Lord, and He will provide. If you need a new car because you've used your old one wisely, and want to donate it to a good ministry, He will provide another. God is a generous giver. He lives by His own rules. If He requires it of you, He will do the same. Believe me.

One last thing I'll mention on that specific verse, is notice how God even provides your seed to sow. You don't have to portion out the "grain" you'd use to make "bread." No, he'll provide extra for you to sow. Make sure you sow it, and don't make the mistake of the man who built barns to store it and stop working (that's no way to abound in good works). This way you will be enriched in every way, so you can be generous in every occasion. That is God's will for your life! When you are living like this, you are walking fully in faith, without even a hint of fear in your life! It's important to remind you that the manna God provided in Exodus 16 was likely as small as the sand. In other words, it blended in with ground meaning what the Israelites gathered each day was hard, tedious work. God would expect us to work hard for His blessings.

Lastly, the key to unlocking this entire Scripture is right at the end: *while you are enriched in everything for all liberality, which causes thanksgiving through us to God.'* The intended focus of your giving is revealed right here. Everything you do should lead to God's glory. Never, ever, ever try to take that glory. If God puts you in a position to give away a billion dollars, you would be better off giving it anonymously than trying to take one ounce of credit. God won't share His glory with anyone. He provides the seed to the sower. Make sure He always gets the glory. He knows how to handle it.

Whenever I think about multiplication, I think about the miracle of the five loaves, and two fish. Jesus took a small boy's lunch and fed well over 5,000 people (there were 5,000 *men* alone.) In John 6:7, Philip even says it would take half a year's wages to feed so many people. It makes sense. If a meal costs three dollars, and there are 5,000 people, that would be $15,000. If there were 10,000 people, it would be $30,000 (Philip was obviously an astute numbers man—my kind of guy.). Jesus didn't even flinch. If God can do it for one, He can do it for 5,000, or 10,000. Take a closer look at what Jesus did though. These verses are extra special to me:

> *'Then Jesus said, "Make the people sit down." Now there was much grass in the place. So the men sat down, in number about five thousand. And Jesus took the loaves, and when He had given thanks He distributed them to the disciples, and the disciples to those sitting down; and likewise of the fish, as much as they wanted. So when they were*

> *filled, He said to His disciples, "Gather up
> the fragments that remain, so that nothing is
> lost."'* **John 6:10-12**

*'And Jesus took the loaves, and when He had given thanks He distributed them to the disciples.'* Jesus gave thanks. Who did He give thanks to? His Father of course! Remember when I said God won't require us to do anything He won't do? Jesus demonstrates this right here. He is thankful. Thankful that a little boy's mother provided his lunch so the glory of God could be demonstrated. Thankful that God provided for all these people, through this humble, little steward. I like to think that Jesus sent the twelve baskets of leftover fish and bread back to the boy's family with him. Even if He didn't, this little boy has an eternally documented memory of his gift to the Lord.

As an aside, I also like the part where Jesus tells them to gather up the fragments so there is no waste.

As I close this chapter, I'd like to leave you with a thought on a slightly different kind of multiplication, but using the same paradigm. Consider that Jesus rarely spoke to great crowds. This instance with the 5,000 men is one. There was another where Jesus fed 4,000 in a similar miracle, and another where He had to stand in a boat so the crowd wouldn't crush Him. But mostly Jesus worked on a personal level. In fact, if you read closely, all of His deepest work was done in the hearts of the twelve disciples. He poured into these men day and night, and led by example. He knew the crowds would receive, and it would be a testimony of God's grace and power through His Son. Yet these crowds, just days after worshipping Him as King of the Jews, screamed for His crucifixion. Jesus poured into the twelve.

He did a good job. It may not have seemed like it at first, when they deserted Him, but all that was in the plan of God. Once Jesus had risen and ascended to Heaven, He sent the Holy Spirit. He changed everything! The Holy Spirit brought to memory everything Jesus had taught the disciples, and enlightened them as to the hidden pearls of wisdom they had seen Jesus live out before their eyes.

So what is my point you may ask? Start small, but start with integrity. Decide on what to do for the Kingdom, and stick to it. Make a decision for God, and release that fear. That fear of money that keeps you in bondage, that fear of giving because you might not have enough. God has promised He provides seed to the sower, *and* bread for eating. Jesus poured His life into twelve ordinary men, who simply had enough integrity that they followed Him regardless of the cost (except for one, who was ultimately replaced by another faithful disciple.) These twelve ordinary men in turn impacted their own circles of influence. And it grew, and grew, and grew until the entire world had changed.

Decide today what you will give. If all you have is a dollar, and you're wondering if that even matters, I can't wait for you to read the next chapter.

# Chapter Nine

# Does My Dollar Really Matter?

In this chapter, I'd like to get down to the practical "nuts and bolts" of giving. We've studied the Scriptures, and spiritual laws, but what if we just feel like we have nothing to give? Many of us have an attitude that because of our struggles, or perhaps because we have little income and are just barely able to give something to the church, and still pay our bills, that one insignificant dollar we might give matters very little in the grand scheme of the Kingdom work of Jesus Christ. I would say to you that it does matter greatly. Remember the story of the widow's mite and how it was not a lot, yet it was *all* she had? You see, it was her heart that Jesus was looking at. As a widow, she had every right to plead for the temple leaders to support her. Instead, she gave her two mites to God, and that shows a pure, giving heart. She gave more than all of the others because she gave it *all*.

> *'41 Now Jesus sat opposite the treasury and saw how the people put money into the treasury. And many who were rich put in much. 42 Then one poor widow came and threw in two mites,[a] which make a quadrans. 43 So He called His disciples to Himself and said to them, "Assuredly, I say to you that this poor widow has put in more than all those who have given to the treasury; 44 for they all put in out of their abundance, but she out of her poverty put in all that she had, her whole livelihood."'*
> **Mark 12:41-44**

Jesus clearly wasn't concerned with the *amount* she put in the treasury. Far more important than that was her heart. Her heart mattered greatly to the Lord. In a sense, our heart is the Lord's greatly sought-after treasure, because if He gets all of our heart, He can use us to change the world, and to also fulfill our full potential. Make no mistake, the desires of your heart matter a great deal to the Lord and He cares for you deeply, but because you can only give a little, this should never stop you from the wonderful act of worship that giving is. Giving will transform you.

Some time ago while on the radio, I took a call from a person who was feeling rather frustrated because she had no money to give. She sincerely desired to give and had hoped she could give a lot more than a tithe. She asked me, "How can you tell us to be faithful givers, which I know is right, when I cannot afford to even put gas in my car to get to work and I am struggling to pay my bills?" I asked her to do me a favor, and the next time she had to put gas in her car, instead of putting $10 worth of gas in her car to put $9.50 in and take the other $.50 and give it to the church. I told her that her car would not miss the $.50 worth of gas and neither would she. I told her God knows her heart and it will be the beginning of a multiplying process which God is faithful to do. I said that her idea of giving seemed insurmountable because she had not yet started to do it. She was unwilling because she felt that $.50 or a dollar was insignificant. It is not insignificant if it is your heart's desire, and the $.50 that you might give is every bit as pleasing to the Lord as the $50 someone else might give, because of the attitude of your heart.

When we think about our money—the management of it and the taking care of those under our roof—when we fear that we won't have enough or that we won't do the right thing with the abundance that we have, we absolutely have to give that fear over to the Lord. Listen to your heart. The Holy Spirit speaks to your heart, and this is why it is so important to pray every day and remain in tune to His voice. Always give as you are able and as your heart desires—not what your checkbook would require nor by a law of your church, and definitely not according to some legalistic mandate you were told is found in the Bible. Rather, give as your heart would desire and as the Lord would lead. Certainly give what is possible, but when it seems there is *nothing* possible for you to give, give anyway knowing there is always something you can do. You may be surprised at how much joy this will bring you. Don't rob yourself of the incredible act of worship giving is.

Friends, it is no secret that we have a difficult time ahead of us yet in this economy. I will admit, I too am fearful—but not about my money. Instead, I am fearful about the lack of giving. I am fearful that the work of Christ will not be able to continue. When I talk about people giving to my ministry, I often say, "If you have an extra dollar, please do not give it to me." Although my ministry needs support, God has continued to provide, and I am grateful to all those who give. But *please* give to the proclamation of the gospel, because ultimately that is our responsibility. Take a great deal of joy in your giving because you give glory to God by supporting your church or one of the great ministries of God, which are proclaiming the gospel. This, my friends, is our primary mission—to insure the gospel is proclaimed.

I have often talked about the American Family Association (AFA.) Over time it is easy to sometimes discount what an organization like this is doing, but let me just recap for you; they are desperately working to put the truth over the airwaves to millions and millions of people in the United States. People like me who would otherwise never have had the opportunity to hear the truth from a biblical perspective. Truth-based perspectives on current events, current politics, and current financial issues.

We know, as our society continues to become more deeply entrenched in a selfish "me" and "my" mentality, there are great organizations like AFA which strive to get the gospel out there. There are other great ministries which are also proclaiming the gospel, and yes, even an organization like Financial Issues Stewardship Ministries which is simply trying to help people to do what is right with God's money so God's work might grow exponentially.

If you want to begin to loose the hold—*the grip*—that your money (*either too much or not enough of it*) has on your life, begin to have an attitude that you cannot take it with you, and the greatest way you can use it is to support the spread of the gospel. It changed *your* life! Why shouldn't it change others' lives? Your church needs it, and Christian ministries need it so that future generations can hear the truth of the gospel. Keep in mind that government authorities or secular organizations will never make sure the truth stays on the air, or insure Christian ministries stay solvent. It is ultimately up to you and I to make sure our *church doors* stay open, and to insure the gospel is proclaimed, and the truth is heard. Relieve your fear by understanding that all that you have, every nickel that you have the ability or the opportunity to earn, whether you go to work joyfully or not, is because God has opened a door for you to provide for your family, earn a living, and provide for the Kingdom.

> *'1 Then the LORD spoke to Moses, saying: "Speak to the children of Israel, that they bring Me an offering. From everyone who gives it willingly with his heart you shall take My offering." '***Exodus 25:1-2**

The Bible makes it very clear—in the Old Testament and the New—we are not to be giving because of some law or mandate to give. Do yourself a favor and read Exodus chapter 25 in full. The Lord makes it clear that the people of Israel, (that represents us today), ought to be giving abundantly, with a willing heart. He does not mention that we ought to be giving our tithe—just 10 percent—*then* give as our heart would lead. Instead, the premise of all of our giving should be as the heart would lead. This means our tithe, and beyond our tithe, our sacrificial giving. Now if you read between the lines in the chapter, you'll notice that in return for asking them to give once, God says three times, He will give to them. When God asks us to give, He has something far greater than we could imagine in store for us. He was asking the Israelites to give to prepare the tabernacle. This tabernacle would house the Law and the Ten Commandments, which would become the foundation for making Israel a great nation. When God asks us to give, it is always, always, *always* to our benefit.

So ultimately, all of our giving ought to be as the Lord leads through our heart's leading, and as we are able. In Deuteronomy 15:7, it says, *'If there is among you a poor man of your brethren, within any of the gates in your land which the LORD your God is giving you, you shall not harden your heart nor shut your hand from your poor brother.'* From a New Testament perspective, could the poor man not only be someone who doesn't have much financially (who we are always called to have compassion on and give to), but also someone who doesn't know the Word of God nor the saving message of the gospel of Jesus Christ?

Certainly the poor man means the brother or sister around us who is poor financially. If however, our heart is not hardened, and our hand is not clenched around all that we have, surely our brother or sister, whether they are spiritually poor or financially poor will be lifted up by us as we are instruments of God's love? As long as there is a willingness in our heart to insure the gospel is proclaimed, and a desire to give freely for the Kingdom of Jesus Christ, we will fulfill Deuteronomy 11:13, which clearly commands us to love the Lord our God and to serve Him with *'all your heart and with all your soul.'*

# Chapter Ten

# The True Tithe

I have heard many times that the New Testament speaks very little of tithing, and that tithing is an Old Testament principle. I agree with this statement. I believe however, there were foreshadows of what the Old Testament tithe represented for the New Testament. In the Old Testament, the laws for tithing were laid out very specifically in several Scriptures. Here is one of the first places the Old Testament mentions tithing:

> *'And all the tithe of the land, whether of the seed of the land or of the fruit of the tree, is the LORD's. It is holy to the LORD.'*
> **Leviticus 27:30**

Tithes were used in several ways. In several places in Deuteronomy 12, God commands the Israelites to take their tithes, offerings, and whatever they had devoted to be holy to the Lord, to a designated place of worship, and celebrate and worship the Lord, having a great time in fellowship and worship. Tithing has always been about joy and building up the community of believers (in this case, the Israelites). It has also been about setting apart something devoted as holy to the Lord.

> '5 "But you shall seek the place where the LORD your God chooses, out of all your tribes, to put His name for His dwelling place; and there you shall go. 6 There you shall take your burnt offerings, your sacrifices, your tithes, the heave offerings of your hand, your vowed offerings, your freewill offerings, and the firstborn of your herds and flocks. 7 And there you shall eat before the LORD your God, and you shall rejoice in all to which you have put your hand, you and your households, in which the LORD your God has blessed you.' **Deuteronomy 12:5-7**

Notice some details between the lines here:

1. God was specifying a place of His choosing for the people to go and worship
2. He was specifying they take their:
    a. Burnt offerings
    b. Sacrifices
    c. Tithes
    d. Special gifts
    e. Freewill offerings and
    f. The firstborn of their herds and flocks
3. He promised the presence of the Lord would be at the place of worship
4. And lastly, He commanded them to rejoice and have a good time because *the Lord had blessed them*

Many Christians I know stop at the 10 percent, but here we see just how much the Israelites were required to give. Under the New Covenant grace of Jesus Christ, it is oh-so-easy to forget that the Old Testament required burnt offerings, sacrifices, freewill offerings, the firstborn of your herds and flocks, AND your tithes. "But Jesus paid the price so we don't have to make sacrifices and burnt offerings" someone might say. I will respond that that's a very astute observation. Now consider firstly what that price was. His very life! Now consider what He requires of you to receive salvation? I'll leave you thinking about that for a few minutes.

Let's take another look at an event we've encountered in a previous chapter: the widow with the two mites.

> *'41 Now Jesus sat opposite the treasury and saw how the people put money into the treasury. And many who were rich put in much. 42 Then one poor widow came and threw in two mites,[a] which make a quadrans. 43 So He called His disciples to Himself and said to them, "Assuredly, I say to you that this poor widow has put in more than all those who have given to the treasury; 44 for they all put in out of their abundance, but she out of her poverty put in all that she had, her whole livelihood."'*
> **Mark 12:41-44**

I believe Jesus was saying here that the widow put more in the treasury than all of the others *combined*. You see, we so often fall into the trap of thinking that God needs our money. Nothing could be further from the truth. If God wanted to, He could touch a multi-billionaire's life in such a way, that he gives everything to the Lord, and begins serving him. And you know what? He has done that in the past! God wants us to give, so we can grow in the things of God, and yes, provide for our community, but He wants us to learn to be like Him—generous and full of faith!

This widow gave out of a pure heart, giving to God all that she had to live on. That's pretty serious. She was basically committing to die, by giving God what she had left. She didn't want to live a few more days from the scraps she could bargain for with a few cents. She gave God *everything* she had to live on (and incidentally, I believe Jesus made sure this widow was taken care of for the rest of her life). If you read closely, Jesus is giving us a clue here as to what He requires of us under the New Covenant.

Now, let's change gears again and go back to the Old Testament commandments on tithing. I have already discussed some of the requirements of the law regarding tithing, and believe me God took obedience very seriously. Take a look at the "discourse" God has (through the prophet Malachi) with the Israelites:

> *'6 "For I am the LORD, I do not change;*
> *Therefore you are not consumed, O sons of*
> *Jacob. 7 Yet from the days of your fathers*
> *You have gone away from My ordinances*
> *And have not kept them. Return to Me, and I*
> *will return to you," Says the LORD of hosts.*
> *"But you said, 'In what way shall we return?'*

*8 "Will a man rob God? Yet you have robbed Me! But you say, 'In what way have we robbed You?' In tithes and offerings. 9 You are cursed with a curse, For you have robbed Me, Even this whole nation.* 10 Bring all the tithes into the storehouse, That there may be food in My house, And try Me now in this," Says the LORD of hosts, "If I will not open for you the windows of heaven And pour out for you such blessing That there will not be room enough to receive it.'* **Malachi 3:6-10** [Emphasis added]

Notice how God says they are under a curse, not that He necessarily cursed them. God always wants to bless us, but if we leave His presence, and step out of obedience to Him, we only hurt ourselves. He makes this very clear in the challenge He issues in verse 10: *'Bring all the tithes into the storehouse, That there may be food in My house, And try Me now in this," Says the LORD of hosts, "If I will not open for you the windows of heaven And pour out for you such blessing That there will not be room enough to receive it.'*

Now think about what God actually said in Deuteronomy 12. *'And there you shall eat before the LORD your God, and you shall rejoice in all to which you have put your hand, you and your households, in which the LORD your God has blessed you.'* I want to show here that God had not placed unreasonable, heavy demands on Israel. In fact, part of what He was saying was they were to use their tithes, offerings, sacrifices etc., to worship in the presence of God, and have a great time with their families. Israel had neglected even doing that! The rest of the chapter in Malachi goes on to say how Israel actually counted it a burden to serve God, and worship in this way.

I believe this attitude is still very present in our churches today. People count it a hardship to give even a portion back to God of what He has given, and bring their offering into His presence with their families and worship. Does God place heavy burdens on us that we can't carry? No, in Matthew 11:29 Jesus explicitly states, *'Take My yoke upon you and learn from Me, for I am gentle and lowly in heart, and you will find rest for your souls.'* Understand what Jesus was saying here.

I want to ask you to pay close attention here, because as I close this chapter, I'm going to tie together all of the concepts I've been talking about, and I really believe it will bless you. Jesus came to earth to fulfill the law, pay the price for our redemption, and show us how to walk as He did.

> *'4 But when the fullness of the time had come,*
> *God sent forth His Son, born of a woman,*

*born under the law, 5 to redeem those who*
*were under the law, that we might receive the*
*adoption as sons.'* **Galatians 4:4-5**

This is wonderful news indeed. There was no way the nation of Israel could ever uphold the entire law. That is why sacrifices and burnt offerings were necessary. What Jesus did, was offer Himself as the ultimate sacrifice, once and for all, to redeem us from *the curse of the law*.

*'13 Christ has redeemed us from the curse of*
*the law, having become a curse for us (for it*
*is written, "Cursed is everyone who hangs*
*on a tree")'* **Galatians 3:13**

Through the power of grace, Jesus allowed us to be adopted back into God's family, and as I've mentioned, actually made us joint-heirs with Himself, as God's royalty. That being said, when discussing Old Testament law, Jesus always places a higher standard on us living under the New Covenant of grace.

See, there is nowhere in the New Testament that tells us Jesus, or any of the writers of the New Testament, ever lowered the expectations or the requirements of the laws of the Old Testament. In fact, Jesus always elevated what was written in the Old Testament. He added on to, or made even a heavier requirement of Old Testament Law. Consider what He says to the Pharisees in the gospel of Luke:

> *'42 "But woe to you Pharisees! For you tithe mint and rue and all manner of herbs, and pass by justice and the love of God. These you ought to have done, without leaving the others undone.'* **Luke 11:42**

And then we know the Old Testament mentions adultery in a very specific way. The religious leaders of Israel were experts in the law, and knew all the so-called "loopholes." So Jesus elevated the law of adultery by saying that even if we lust with our eyes we have committed adultery. In the Scripture above, He simply says you shouldn't have neglected the tithe, but I believe it is clear He is far more interested in their *heart's* condition. Can you imagine if He decided to talk about percentages of our giving? He might have said that the Old Testament law requires 10 percent, but I tell you that 10 percent is just a beginning. And he may have gone on to require a great deal more. In fact, I think He does:

> *'9 that if you confess with your mouth the Lord Jesus and believe in your heart that God has raised Him from the dead, you will be saved. 10* **For with the heart one believes unto righteousness,** *and with the mouth confession is made unto salvation.'* **Romans 10:9-10** *[Emphasis added]*

The apostle Paul says it here in black and white. It is with the heart that we believe and are justified. God is concerned about our heart, more than a relatively crude set of laws (the Bible refers to the law that way, compared to grace). Now, here is the crux of the chapter—notice what the confession requirement is: *"If you declare with your mouth, "Jesus is Lord."* We have to declare Jesus our Lord. Every Christian knows this, but you may be seeing this in a new light right now. It means that essentially everything you own and everything you *are* belongs to your Lord. That's why we say we *give our life* to Christ. The second part of the verse is also crucial; *"and believe in your heart that God raised him from the dead, you will be saved."* You have to believe in your heart—that means behave as though Jesus is alive and is your Lord! Because He is most definitely alive.

So now we finally get back to the event of the widow with the two mites. I believe Jesus used that opportunity to show us what is required under the covenant of grace. We are to give it *all* to Him. That, my friends, is the **true tithe**. He wants it all—our heart, our motives, our effort, our trust—all of it should be for God. Why? So God can hoard it up? Of course not. So He can bless you!

> *'23 And whatever you do, do it heartily, as to the Lord and not to men, 24 knowing that from the Lord you will receive the reward of the inheritance; for you serve the Lord Christ.'* **Colossians 3:23-24**

Now there still may be some question of "How do I give it all to God? Does that mean give all of my money away?" As I mentioned earlier, that is not what I'm saying. I believe God wants our hearts because that is the most effective and efficient way to get Kingdom work done. The most effective way to insure your heart is in the right place, is to be sure you're praying, reading the Word, and remaining sensitive to the Holy Spirit's voice. He'll tell you what you need to give, where you need to give, and how. These Scriptures can't say it more clearly:

*'For as many as are led by the Spirit of God,
these are sons of God.'* **Romans 8:14**


*'But if you are led by the Spirit, you are not
under the law.'* **Galatians 5:18**


You must be led by the Holy Spirit daily in your giving. When you hear His sweet and gentle voice, you can't go wrong! You will automatically be overjoyed to give, and help others. His presence will fill you, empower you, and give you a whole new perspective on everything. He will give you hope, and show you that sowing into God's Kingdom is the best investment you'll ever make.

To close this chapter, look at this example of New Testament giving. I believe everything I've discussed in this chapter is represented by this example. This is the model we should attain to, and epitomizes the completely devoted heart of the New Covenant giver:


*'42 And they continued steadfastly in the apostles' doctrine and fellowship, in the breaking of bread, and in prayers. 43 Then fear came upon every soul, and many wonders and signs were done through the*

*apostles. 44 Now all who believed were together, and had all things in common, 45 and sold their possessions and goods, and divided them among all, as anyone had need. 46 So continuing daily with one accord in the temple, and breaking bread from house to house, they ate their food with gladness and simplicity of heart, 47 praising God and having favor with all the people. And the Lord added to the church[a] daily those who were being saved. '***Acts 2:42-47***

## Chapter Eleven

# Through the Eye of a Needle

So far we've spoken at length about getting our heart into the right place, concerning our finances. I would hope that everyone now understands that compartmentalizing our money away from God is one of the most detrimental things we can do to our growth in Christ. It simply shows we don't trust God as we say we do, and in fact, we haven't given Him our lives as we claim. To recap, money represents a huge portion of our time and work effort. It's just a symbol. We belong to God, and all of our increase is because of Him.

Okay, now with that foundation soundly laid, we can dive into some deeper stuff. Some of us may recall the verse in Luke 18:25 which is used frequently out of context: *'For it is easier for a camel to go through the eye of a needle than for a rich man to enter the kingdom of God.* "' Why would we place any emphasis whatsoever on wealth if it is so difficult for this rich man to enter the Kingdom of Heaven? After all, we know how difficult it is going to be, under normal circumstances, for us to walk and live the Christian faith. Certainly, I don't want to be too wealthy and eliminate my possibility at all, right? So, maybe I should just give away all the money that I earn, so that I can be assured of an entrance into the Kingdom of God? Well, I imagine that's a bit of an exaggeration of what we may sometimes think, though I am certain entire cults have been formed around that principle. Take a look at the following Scripture before I answer those questions:

> '13 For everyone who partakes only of milk
> is unskilled in the word of righteousness,
> for he is a babe. 14 But solid food belongs
> to those who are of full age, that is, those
> who by reason of use have their senses
> exercised to discern both good and evil.'
> **Hebrews 5:13-14**

The writer of Hebrews is saying here that there are mature and immature believers. Those who are immature tend to not want to put the time, effort, and devotion into understanding the deeper mysteries of the gospel. I am confident, however, that you are a mature believer and will grab what I am about to say completely, without confusion. What I am about to discuss is getting into some "meat" so I hope you enjoy a good "Word steak!"

To understand Jesus' statement about how difficult it is for a rich man to go through the eye of a needle, we have to go back to the teaching on the heart. The heart is the key to understanding how to approach your finances, wealth and treasures. That being said, I ask, "Is having great wealth ok?" (That means money, right here on earth.)  I think God has given many people the ability to earn money. Let me explain. Ask yourself *"If it wasn't for wealth and abundance and for the blessings beyond what God provides for us to live daily, how could the Kingdom of Jesus Christ ever be financed?"* How could we possibly see the proclamation of the Gospel to the ends of the earth if we do not have income or finances to assure that the Gospel can be, or is, proclaimed? I am not saying God needs us to accomplish His goals, but we are His instruments here on earth.

In fact, to back up my statement, take a look at this Scripture:

*'17 then you say in your heart, 'My power and the might of my hand have gained me this wealth.'*

*18 "And you shall remember the LORD your God, for it is He who gives you power to get wealth, that He may establish His covenant which He swore to your fathers, as it is this day.'* **Deuteronomy 8:17-18**

Now do you see why you need to be mature to understand this Scripture? On one hand, Jesus is telling us how difficult it is for a rich man to enter Heaven. On the other, God is saying He is giving us power to get wealth and in fact, it is a sin to say we have gained it ourselves. If you've ever seen a "meaty" Scripture, this is one. I want you to notice two very interesting details in this Scripture; first—God reminds us to keep our hearts pure, and not be conceited, as if we had anything to do with our power to get wealth. Second—God says this wealth confirms His covenant with our ancestors. This means our spiritual ancestors, and as I mentioned earlier in the book, Christ took this covenant, made a better one, and made us joint heirs with Him. This Scripture clearly shows that the wealth God gives us is intended to further His Kingdom!

So with this Scripture in mind, I think it is very clear in Jesus'' statement in Luke, that He is indicating how easy it is for a wealthy person to depend upon his or her riches. Such a person wants to rely on their (seeming) own ability, which is the desire and the need to earn a living or make money. Jesus knew all too well how difficult it was for someone to turn away from riches to find salvation. He understood how dependent we can be, and how much love we could have for wealth, or for the ability to earn or make money. Money in this world, seems to be security and success. Jesus understood that all of this would lead to pride in such a way that our emphasis would be on what we have done personally—what we have accomplished, not on what God has done through us.

It is very difficult for a wealthy person who believes they have accomplished all they've done purely out of their own strength, and because of who they are, not because of who God is. This makes it very difficult for them to find eternal life and salvation because they are looking at their riches through a worldly perspective. They don't give God the glory, but solely trust in their riches. When a person reaches a state of wealth without acknowledging God, it becomes very difficult—not impossible however—to be willing to give it all up (not literally) and humbly acknowledge God with their entire life.

One significant difference we see between heart conditions in Luke 18 is when our heart is right we can see the Lord bringing us wealth, because we are devoting it to His kingdom. The Lord is kind and just however, and brings wealth to the ungodly through honest means as well (God never approves of nor endorses unjust gain of course.). The ungodly simply don't acknowledge it. Obviously, the rich man who places his wealth first and foremost in his life will never see the Kingdom of Heaven. In fact, he *worships* his wealth! This is what Paul means in the following Scripture:

> *'For the love of money is a root of all kinds of evil, for which some have strayed from the faith in their greediness, and pierced themselves through with many sorrows.'*
> **1 Timothy 6:10**

Notice the difference between a godly person and an ungodly person. The ungodly person *'strayed from the faith in their greediness.'* We should instead, be eager for God and His kingdom, then He can trust us with increase because He knows we will fund His work, and money won't corrupt us. In all that we are, and in all that we do and all that we have, we are to understand where it all came from, why we have it, and what it could accomplish for the Kingdom of Jesus Christ.

I have often told the story of a wealthy man I know. He gives millions of dollars a year to Kingdom work. He has often said to me that God has given him no talents, no gifts, no abilities, except for one—to earn money. He believes that it is his obligation to continue to earn money so that he can continue to give his surplus for the proclamation of the Gospel. In his opinion, that is how he is being a good steward of the gospel of Jesus Christ. So I know without a doubt there are many very wealthy people who will enter the gates of Heaven hearing the words, *"Well done, good and faithful servant."*

Someone might ask, *"What about the verses where Jesus says that we are not to lay up treasures for ourselves on earth? Obviously, He must mean that we should not be saving our money and certainly not investing it in the stock market or mutual funds or IRAs or 401Ks, or any other income-producing vehicle. We should be giving all of it so that we can be assured that we have no treasures, right?"*

Well, certainly in Matthew 6:19, the Lord makes it clear that we should focus on Heavenly treasure, and not earthly treasure. As a matter of fact, I wrote a book on estate planning around the idea of this verse. It says, *'19 "Do not lay up for yourselves treasures on earth, where moth and rust destroy and where thieves break in and steal; 20 but lay up for yourselves treasures in heaven, where neither moth nor rust destroys and where thieves do not break in and steal.'* Finally, verse 21 gets to the heart of the matter. *'For where your treasure is, there your heart will be also.'*

We need to pay close attention to this verse, and if you don't have it underlined in your Bible, I would suggest that you do that. You see, it is about your heart. What is your heart's condition regarding storing up treasures? Are you storing up treasure because you have worked hard for it, and you believe you ought to hoard it and save it for a rainy day? Are you trusting your treasures to get you through the next year, or five years? Or are you depending upon the Lord? Are you laying up this treasure so that you might have ease and comfort in your retirement, or are you depending upon the Lord for your ease and comfort in your retirement? Consider again, the following Scripture which I believe to be one of the most important of this book:

> *'33 But seek first the kingdom of God and His righteousness, and all these things shall be added to you. 34 Therefore do not worry about tomorrow, for tomorrow will worry about its own things. Sufficient for the day is its own trouble.'* **Matthew 6:33-34**

I believe that seeking God's Kingdom first can assure comfort so that we may serve the King in a greater way. What I mean by this is that with the money with which we have been blessed—whether it creates a little wealth or a lot of wealth—we should grow it and not bury it in the ground for a "rainy day." Again, we should not grow our finances so that our heart trusts in our wealth, but to grow it so that our treasures might do a mighty work for the Kingdom of God. It is our heart that needs to be focused and our treasure must be to seek and save the lost—to see the Kingdom of Jesus Christ grow. We certainly are not to be laying up treasures for the sake of security outside of God.

I would like to say, regarding saving money here on earth, in Proverbs 13:22, and 2 Corinthians 12:14, it would certainly appear that parents are to save for their children to provide a stable future. It is not sinful to have assets such as insurance and retirement plans, savings accounts, and trust funds. We should be saving and trying to be prepared for what lies ahead and for our future. Proverbs 15:22 says, "Without counsel, plans go awry, but in the multitude of counselors they are established." If we are planning we are likely saving and I believe we should.

But we are still to trust the Lord will provide for us and our children, and give His Kingdom the highest priority. I always like to remind people that one way God provides is that he gives us the intellect, opportunity, and common sense to prepare. God will, without a doubt, insure our children are taken care of if we serve Him faithfully, but remember there is a part that we have to play.

*'A good man leaves an inheritance to his children's children, But the wealth of the sinner is stored up for the righteous.'*
**Proverbs 13:22**

*'Now for the third time I am ready to come to you. And I will not be burdensome to you; for I do not seek yours, but you. For the children ought not to lay up for the parents, but the parents for the children.'*
**2 Corinthians 12:14**

In closing this chapter, I want to focus on the following Scripture:

*'No one can serve two masters; for either he will hate the one and love the other, or he will be devoted to the one and despise the other. You cannot serve God and money.'*
**Matthew 6:24 (ESV)**

Remember, we have to consider this Scripture with spiritual maturity, and discernment. Again, it is the intentions of our heart which matter. You can be a righteous steward of wealth, but not serve money itself. If you seek God's Kingdom first, and devote your life to financing or performing His work, you will never be enslaved by money. If however, you begin to trust in the money, and allow yourself to become deceived by wealth, and begin to focus on earthly comforts, you will be serving money. In fact, wealthy believers have to remain ever-vigilant against this trap. If you think you can serve two masters however, you are dreaming. Trust me— there will be a time when the two masters you are serving will make opposing demands on you and on each other. The key is to remain in daily relationship with the Lord through prayer, Bible study, and fellowship with believers. On the other hand, one cannot sit back, make poor choices and not save or make an attempt to be a good steward and just wait for God to provide. Chances are He has provided and you did nothing with it or did not recognize the provision.

So in summary, we need to understand that a biblical world-view of our investments will insure that we are investing in our Lord Jesus Christ. If we give ourselves to our work, to a collection, or hoarding of money, we will begin to take great enjoyment in material objects. Those things may give us temporary enjoyment in this world, but the pleasure will be fleeting. Instead, we are investing in the Kingdom of

Heaven—this should always be our first and only focus. In fact, even saving for our children's future is an investment in the Kingdom, because when coupled with raising them in the Lord's ways, we will be laying a foundation to continue a legacy of supporting Kingdom work. It is in Christ that we are giving ourselves first and foremost.

# Chapter Twelve

# Without Financial Security, How Can I Serve God?

I know so many Christians who tell themselves, "Well, I'm only hoarding my money so that I can ultimately serve God in a better and more powerful way." Many of them began very sincerely in the beginning, but remember what we talked about in the last chapter? At some point, everyone will have to make a choice between serving money and God. Note that this problem does not apply only to the rich, or those with money to save. In fact, it is just as easy to put off submitting your finances to God when you have very little.

Please don't kid yourself into believing that you are hoarding, saving, and growing your wealth so that *someday* you can serve God. Maybe that is true, and maybe that will even happen, but there is a great risk that what Jesus calls "the deceitfulness of richness" could begin to creep in. Even though you've wrapped this idea in this veil of Christ-centeredness, money is something to be treated extremely cautiously. A simple way to always keep sight of Christ in your finances is to give away some of your overflow, and some of your wealth while you are saving (Remember He gives seed to the sower. Never hoard your seed.).

And again, let's never lose sight of the fact that Jesus Christ is the great Multiplier. The Bible clearly tells us that. We need to continually give so that we might continually have as we've discussed in previous chapters. A dam that never gets replenished becomes stagnant and dead, but a river is constantly moving, and living things thrive in it. Now again, I know that sounds a bit like the "prosperity preaching," which I despise, but there is truth in believing that God will continue to provide—sometimes in a great and powerful way for those that continue to provide for Kingdom work today. The difference is exactly what I mentioned earlier— the focus. Focus on His kingdom first, and His righteousness and all these things will be given to you (as you need them, I would clarify).

A part of financial integrity is we are also to work hard in whatever gifts and talents God has given us. It appears that today's younger generation seems to display a diminishing work ethic. When my wife and I committed to praying for our daughters' husbands, we prayed three things. First, we prayed that they would love the Lord more than anything else. Second, we prayed they would love our daughters as Christ loves the Church. And, third, we prayed that they would have a good and strong work ethic. We knew that if we prayed these three things that all the other things would fall into place. And praise be to God we were correct!

> *'Let him who stole steal no longer, but rather let him labor, working with his hands what is good, that he may have something to give him who has need.'* **Ephesians 4:28**

In the Scripture above, Paul makes it very clear that a man ought to, instead of stealing, steal no more. He also makes the case that we should have a strong work ethic. See, it's through earthly work that we can do "Kingdom" work. It's through the work of our hands, that we can feed the needy, and we can see that the gospel is proclaimed. Never forget that Jesus was first a carpenter, and I am sure a committed and hard working one. As Christians, we ought to earn enough to share some of our earnings with the needy. I don't believe that Ephesians 4:28 is merely a call to stop stealing, or a just call to stop being greedy. I believe that the idea of this Scripture is that we need to be generous. Is it is a mandate of generosity to have a changed attitude toward our work? I believe that is certainly part of it.

So now, what about this idea of financial security, or retirement, or eventually living in ease? Does God have anything to say about that? I think Paul answers that question in the following Scripture:

*6 Now godliness with contentment is great gain. 7 For we brought nothing into this world, and it is certain [c] we can carry nothing out. 8 And having food and clothing, with these we shall be content. 9 But those who desire to be rich fall into temptation and a snare, and into many foolish and harmful lusts which drown men in destruction and perdition. 10 For the love of money is a root of all kinds of evil, for which some have strayed from the faith in their greediness, and pierced themselves through with many sorrows.*

*11 But you, O man of God, flee these things and pursue righteousness, godliness, faith, love, patience, gentleness. 12 Fight the good fight of faith, lay hold on eternal life, to which you were also called and have confessed the good confession in the presence of many witnesses. 13 I urge you in the sight of God who gives life to all things, and before Christ Jesus who witnessed the good confession before Pontius Pilate, 14 that you keep this commandment without spot, blameless until our Lord Jesus Christ's appearing, 15 which He will manifest in His own time, He who is the blessed and only Potentate, the King of kings and Lord of lords, 16 who alone has immortality, dwelling in unapproachable light, whom no man has seen or can see, to whom be honor and everlasting power. Amen.*

*17 Command those who are rich in this present age not to be haughty, nor to trust in uncertain riches but in the living God, who gives us richly all things to enjoy. 18 Let them do good, that they be rich in good works, ready to give, willing to share, 19 storing up for themselves a good foundation for the time to come, that they may lay hold on eternal life.'* **1 Timothy 6:3-19**

I think that throughout this letter to Timothy, Paul is giving his disciple (and giving us) some ideas of standards for the Christian life that we should be using as a foundation to build on and striving to attain. These may be significant lifestyle changes for some of us. That doesn't mean we should be any less earnest in making the necessary adjustments. I believe this section is a very specific answer to the question of "What about financial security?" Remember that people weren't very different 2,000 years ago than what they are today. The Holy Spirit is present on the earth and convicts us of the destructive paths Satan would try to lead us into. It is a clear statement that living the Christian lifestyle leads to a far greater gain, as opposed to hoarding or storing away our money for our financial security—even though we need to plan. We need to find balance. I will explain this balance in more detail later in this chapter.

We have heard so many times that we don't see the U-Haul truck behind the hearse. We brought nothing into the world and we can take nothing out. Does that mean that we don't make provisions for our children? Of course we do. Does that mean that we shouldn't make long-term provisions for the ministries we support? Of course we should. Obviously, we ought to be using wisdom to save and plan so that some of those things are accomplished. That is different than hoarding for who knows what. But along the way, along the road of our Christian walk, one of our primary focuses should be providing for some of those in need. Those in need of material necessities, in need of the gospel and ministries in need of financial support.

I love what Paul says to his young disciple Timothy, about contentment: *"But godliness with contentment is great gain."* We cannot go through our life lacking contentment, believing our contentment will come from having more food, more clothing, or more material things. Such thinking is a deception. It is an extremely powerful deception. Here's why: the model of selfish hoarding undermines the law of sowing and reaping. Those who strive to gain contentment by seeking worldly "comforts" rarely sow righteousness and are always chasing the wind. They will never reap contentment because contentment is found in the knowledge that we are temporary travelers in this world. We were not created to live here eternally.

> *'Beloved, I beg you as sojourners and pilgrims, abstain from fleshly lusts which war against the soul,'* **1 Peter 2:11**

It may be a difficult concept to grasp with the influence of modern society's worship of instant gratification, and excess, but there is a reason we are to find fulfillment in the fact that we have just food and clothes. Remember, verse 9 of the letter to 1 Timothy 6 says, *But those who desire to be rich fall into temptation and a snare, and into many foolish and harmful lusts which drown men in destruction and perdition.'* The temptation to lust after a seeming life of comfort is based on an elaborate illusion. Almost all of the television shows, magazines, and even much radio glorifies "making it" and hitting the "big time." It becomes an ingrained desire within us from the time we are old enough to talk. The Word of God however, says that He will provide for us, and if we simply have food and clothes we should be content. Remember He provides opportunities to earn a living, our talents, a strong back, time, two hands on and on. Remembering this reduces our natural desires to the most basic elements of survival in this world. For anything more we should have an attitude of, if God gives it to us, we will be overjoyed, praise Him for it, and give it back to Him in some way. Tim Tebow is a good example of praising God for the opportunity and talent. He gets mocked because the world can't grasp that. If all else fails for Tebow what will really matter is that when he speaks he will be able to fill every seat in an auditorium to share his testimony and to share the gospel. God already knows the kid that will come to the Lord as a result. That is receiving prosperity.

When we understand that God is our provider and may even choose to lead us through a time of material scarcity for His own infinitely deep purposes, or to grow us, we will be content with whatever we have. This is in exact contrast to the world's illusion of contentment.

Paul also makes it very clear that we are to guard and protect our true contentment against these seductive illusions of becoming rich. Because of our fallen human nature and pride, these enchanting desires can quickly become a snare if we allow them into our heart, and we will, as a result, fall into foolish and worthless pursuits that could very well lead to our spiritual and physical destruction. This is a very serious thought, and one way to counter it is with Peter's nugget of wisdom: Always remember you are an alien in this world. A foreigner, temporarily working here to save the lost. Why hoard up comforts here? You should be focusing on your eternal life. When you adjust your frame of reference to this eternal context, it becomes easy to understand the Scripture in Matthew 6 we have already discussed where Jesus commands, *"But seek first his kingdom and his righteousness, and all these things will be given to you as well. Therefore do not worry about tomorrow, for tomorrow will worry about itself. Each day has enough trouble of its own."* Just seek the Kingdom. That's all you need to do. Frame everything in this context, and you will find contentment. God will never let His servants, nor their families, lack any good thing. Believe that. Become His faithful servant.

Now to balance our case with wisdom, and get to some "meat." It might appear that by verse 9 in the Scripture above, Paul is stating that to have an abundance, or to wisely save and invest our money is such foolishness, we should avoid it at all costs. I don't believe Paul is saying that *at all*—not because it's my opinion, but because of what he says in verse 10. He says, "For the *LOVE* of money" [Emphasis added]. I emphasize again the word '...*LOVE of money is a root of all kinds of evil, for which some have strayed from the faith in their greediness, and pierced themselves through with many sorrows.'* Paul is clearly saying that it is not money itself; it is not working hard to earn more money that is the problem here, whether it be through investment strategies, savings, or through good old-fashioned elbow grease.

The problem occurs when *money* becomes the *master* which we serve. This is when we will experience many sorrows. Our master is that which we love, and pursue above all else. We should look at verse 9 as a warning from God. We should look at verse 10 as the reason He is giving us the warning. The love of money will lead to many sorrows.

I believe that a proper biblical world-view for all areas of our wealth rests upon verses 17 through 19. These are verses that we would be well-served to remember and pray through, and to think about often, as we go about our normal daily activities in earning a living. It simply says this, '*17*

*Command those who are rich in this present age not to be haughty, nor to trust in uncertain riches but in the living God, who gives us richly all things to enjoy. 18 Let them do good, that they be rich in good works, ready to give, willing to share, 19 storing up for themselves a good foundation for the time to come, that they may lay hold on eternal life.'*

Paul instructs us not to trust in material things, but to put all our faith and trust in a living God. See, it goes on to say that it is He who gives us all of these things that we are enjoying. It is not us who have this incredible talent and ability to get all these things, but it is God who gives them to us. So, it is in Him that we are to put our trust. It does not say, *"Hey, Timothy, make sure you tell them to get rid of all their riches. Make sure that you tell them that being wealthy is a sin... that being wealthy is wrong."* He is not saying that at all. He is saying that we should be content with food and clothes, and if God gives us more than this we should be exceptionally joyful and thankful, and determine to seek how the Lord would have us give back to Him for so graciously blessing us.

Paul is also reminding those of us who are fortunate enough to have some savings set aside for our retirement, to do good with those savings. And here is the part I like. It is found in verse 18: *"and to be generous and willing to share."* See, we have to be ready for when the Lord calls us and speaks to our hearts; we need to be ready to give away some of what we have. We must be able to hear His voice, though. The only way that is possible is through daily relationship with Him. In fact, without that, we are in danger of falling prey to the lethal seduction of the illusion of earthly riches. We need to be ready, even though we are storing it up, or growing it to invest into a good cause, to give it away, so that as Paul says in verse 19, *'storing up for themselves a good foundation for the time to come, that they may lay hold on eternal life.'*

Saving up for our financial security, and for our pensions for our retirement, or for our children is not a bad thing, as long as it remains in the perspective of a biblical world-view of eternity, and not the secular world-view of wealth.

# Chapter Thirteen

# Are We Under a Legal Responsibility to Give?

I would like to start this chapter out by first discussing the context of the Mosaic Law, as related to the Word of God and biblical history. The law was given to the nation of Israel because there were no concrete guidelines for what was and wasn't sin, up to that point. Certain sins were obvious, such as Cain murdering Abel. I'm pretty confident Abel would have liked to keep on living for a good while, but other sins are not as clear-cut. For example, who would bear the cost if your cow wandered onto my land, but your shepherds killed my cow?

It is therefore easy to see the need for laws, but a problem arises because there is a new focal point for how we should live. The focal point of course, is the law. This is a very long, detailed discussion but in short, the nation of Israel came to practically worship the law, instead of the Giver of the law. There is a huge difference. The religious leaders throughout the Old Testament, in Jesus' time, and even many in the apostles' time used their expert knowledge of the law as a seeming moral high ground to try to establish that they were better than the common sinners and law breakers. The law, to them, became an idol.

Another problem with the law was that it is a very crude representation of a better, heavenly paradigm. What this means is that the law was the equivalent of sending a text message to your wife saying "I love you" as opposed to planning a romantic dinner, having her buy a new, expensive dress, picking her up in a limousine and spending a wonderful evening together. In fact, the difference between those two examples doesn't come close to how much better the heavenly version is of what the law represents. It is beyond the scope of this chapter, but I highly recommend you read the whole of Hebrews 8 to understand, and see for yourself, how this works with the old and new covenants as well.

Another problem with the law is that it can actually ignite a desire for sin. In many cases, we would not have known what certain sins were, had they not been explicitly explained to us. Then we want to start thinking about them, and desire can take root in us. *"Heresy!"* religious people might shout. But that is what Paul explains in Romans 7:

> *'7What shall we say then? Is the law sin? Certainly not! On the contrary, I would not have known sin except through the law. For I would not have known covetousness unless the law had said, "You shall not covet." 8 But sin, taking opportunity by the commandment, produced in me all manner of evil desire. For apart from the law sin was dead. 9 I was alive once without the law, but when the commandment came, sin revived and I died. 10 And the commandment, which was to bring life, I found to bring death. 11 For sin, taking occasion by the commandment, deceived me, and by it killed me. 12 Therefore the law is holy, and the commandment holy and just and good.'* **Romans 7:7-12**

The problem of course, lies within us. The law is definitely holy, but we are fallen, corrupt and unspiritual. The law is spiritual, and when you are operating in the presence of the Holy Spirit, the law is a beautiful thing. Because you can truly understand it in His presence. The law reveals those better heavenly realities. We just can't grasp without the help of the Holy Spirit because we are spiritually dead without Him. The Holy Spirit is also called the Spirit of Christ, and in fact, Jesus even said this in John 15:5, *'"I am the vine, you are the branches. He who abides in Me, and I in him, bears much fruit; for without Me you can do nothing.'*

Paul goes on in verse 14 of Romans 7 to say what I've been explaining, *'For we know that the law is spiritual, but I am carnal, sold under sin.'* So the bottom line is that the law is still holy, and good. However, it is a relatively crude teacher for unspiritual, sinful people. Thank God that He provided a better way through Jesus Christ!

Okay, now it's a little easier to see how and why Jesus placed a heavier requirement on the commandments, as we discussed in a previous chapter. He was saying that the religious leaders should have been striving to completely fulfill the law without neglecting love and compassion. The little secret between the lines (that I believe the Holy Spirit will show you if you allow Him) is that anyone trying to uphold the law would realize two things very quickly: (1) It is impossible to uphold the law on your own, and (2) There are many cases where keeping to the strict letter of the law would seemingly contradict what should be a loving response to a situation. If a person honestly strived to keep the law, and love their fellow human being, there would only be one way to do it. I believe the reconciliation of these two realizations would lead a person to (1) Realize they are a hopeless sinner and in no place to judge anyone, and (2) Realize they must entirely humble themselves before God to try to keep all of the commandments as best as possible. Let's look at a perfect example:

*'1 But Jesus went to the Mount of Olives. 2 Now early[a] in the morning He came again into the temple, and all the people came to Him; and He sat down and taught them. 3 Then the scribes and Pharisees brought to Him a woman caught in adultery. And when they had set her in the midst, 4 they said to Him, "Teacher, this woman was caught in adultery, in the very act. 5 Now Moses, in the law, commanded us that such should be stoned. But what do You say?" 6 This they said, testing Him, that they might have something of which to accuse Him. But Jesus stooped down and wrote on the ground with His finger, as though He did not hear.*

*7 So when they continued asking Him, He raised Himself up and said to them, "He who is without sin among you, let him throw a stone at her first." 8 And again He stooped down and wrote on the ground. 9 Then those who heard it, being convicted by their conscience, went out one by one, beginning with the oldest even to the last. And Jesus was left alone, and the woman standing in the midst. 10 When Jesus had raised Himself up and saw no one but the woman, He said to her, "Woman, where are those accusers of yours? Has no one condemned you?" 11 She said, "No one, Lord." And Jesus said to her, "Neither do I condemn you; go and sin no more."'* **John 8:1-11**

Most Christians know this true story but in my opinion, the deeper subtext is lost on most. I believe the doctrine of grace is perfectly illustrated and summarized by Jesus right here. Make no mistake—this woman was a sinner. I'm not sure if she was married, or if the man she was sinning with was married, or both, but either way, a spouse or spouses somewhere were being brutally betrayed. Jesus responded with unprecedented wisdom and grace. This is how we should approach the question *"Are we under a legal responsibility to give?"*

What I mean is that no one can judge you for not giving, because of Romans 3:23; *"...for all have sinned and fall short of the glory of God."* The only One who can judge, chooses not to—until the end of the age when it is necessary. So you have freedom. Again, as you might have guessed, it's about the heart. Certainly there are Scriptures in even the New Testament, where the apostles admonish believers to give, support ministry, and give generously, but the request is not based in the law. Instead, as we see in the following Scripture, the heart is the focus. When God has your heart, He has everything He needs to help you fulfill any legal requirements.

> *'6 But this I say: He who sows sparingly will also reap sparingly, and he who sows bountifully will also reap bountifully. 7 So let each one give as he purposes in his heart, not grudgingly or of necessity; for God loves a cheerful giver.'* **2 Corinthians 9:6-7**

The apostle Paul simply says it as it stands—as much as you give is to the degree you allow God to bless you. We don't give to receive, but the law of sowing and reaping is undeniable. In my humble opinion, this takes care of legalism right here. It's a heart thing.

I would also like to point out that Paul says, '*So let each one give as he purposes in his heart.*' We saw this Scripture in a previous chapter. The word *heart* is right there in black and white. If that's not a clue, I don't know what is. Paul is also saying you should determine beforehand what you are going to give. Spend some time on it. Now for the kicker in verse 7—'*...not grudgingly or of necessity; for God loves a cheerful giver.*' I believe this adequately answers the question in our chapter title: *Are we under a legal responsibility to give?* No, we clearly are not under an obligation or legal responsibility to give, but let's look at *why* we aren't under *necessity* or compulsion.

See, the idea is that God loves a cheerful giver, and it becomes extremely difficult for us to be thinking about our giving to the Kingdom if we are giving under some sort of law. Giving is one of the most incredible acts of worship. We don't want to be giving because our pastor has told us that we *have* to give—as a biblical mandate, or even that we need to give a certain percentage because it is expected of us. We need to give because *God* tells us that we should give, and we should be madly, head-over-heels in love with God and trust to do whatever He asks. I don't think God wants us to worship Him because we are forced to, that is not worship at all.

Paul is reminding us here that we should want to give and desire to give. We should want to give as our heart purposes, and as the Lord leads us. Again, when the Lord has our heart, this whole topic of legal requirements in fact becomes a non-issue. If we give out of love to the Lord, and as we plan or purpose in our heart, it will create in us a cheerful attitude toward giving. I believe Paul is reminding us that there is a grace in giving earnestly. If we allow it, grace bears rich fruit in us of deep love for the Lord and the desire to see His Kingdom grow. It is because He loved us first, and lovingly pardoned us like the woman caught in adultery, that we can cheerfully give back to such a wonderful Savior. If we will excel in that grace of giving, God is faithful in His blessings to us. My wife and I are so blessed by our Church that we literally can't wait to worship through our giving; it almost feels selfish to get such joy from it.

> *'10 Now may He who supplies seed to the sower, and bread for food, supply and multiply the seed you have sown and increase the fruits of your righteousness, 11 while you are enriched in everything for all liberality, which causes thanksgiving through us to God. 12 For the administration of this service not only supplies the needs of the saints, but also is abounding through many thanksgivings to God.'* **2 Corinthians 9:10-12**

We've seen this Scripture before and again we see that God is certainly the great Multiplier, but one of the most important parts of these verses that we seem to forget is the beginning of verse 10, *"Now may He who supplies seed to the sower..."* Listen, if we go through our life being the sower—if we are giving and if we are doing all we can to see the Kingdom of Christ grow, and that the Gospel of Him is proclaimed—as sowers, we are sowing not money but the Word of God.

We are doing all that we can through our giving to see that the Good News of the gospel is proclaimed. It reminds us that God is the One who provides us with the ability to do that. If we are going to be a cheerful giver and not give out of compulsion or a mandate, but give out of compassion and generosity; out of the goodness of our hearts, then we need to understand that the seed He has given us to sow will be multiplied. Even that in itself is worth getting cheerful about.

To wrap this chapter up, I think the following Scripture summarizes the gist of what I'm trying to say:

> *'28 Come to Me, all you who labor and are heavy laden, and I will give you rest. 29 Take My yoke upon you and learn from Me, for I am gentle and lowly in heart, and you will find rest for your souls. 30 For My yoke is easy and My burden is light.''* **Matthew 11:28-30**

Jesus placed on us a heavier requirement than the law because He wants us to depend on Him. In Him, even a heavier requirement becomes a piece of cake. He wants us to learn of Him. He's gentle, and meek. He promises us rest for our souls. I love this Scripture because it carries such a sense of relief. Our giving should never be out of legal obligation. Legal obligation, like the law, can kill us. To the unspiritual it is cold, heartless, and cruel. Jesus is meek, loving, and gentle. The Spirit of Jesus—the Holy Spirit is right here on earth. He has been here permanently for over 2,000 years, and He and Jesus are One. When we come to rely on the Holy Spirit, we will know where and how to give. It will be a pleasure, not a burden. Our weariness will be removed, and He will show us how to have rest in Him. And the Kingdom will effortlessly grow.

# Chapter Fourteen

# Is Sacrificial Giving Burdensome Giving?

You know, it is remarkable how many sermons I have heard about giving that never mention what a person should do when they have almost nothing to give. I think many church leaders try to sidestep this controversial issue, but I believe it really needs to be addressed. When you read the gospels you see Jesus using various parables to emphasize the importance of giving, as well as real life instructions to certain people He encounters. One of these is the parable of the talents:

'24 *"Then he who had received the one talent came and said, 'Lord, I knew you to be a hard man, reaping where you have not sown, and gathering where you have not scattered seed. 25 And I was afraid, and went and hid your talent in the ground. Look, there you have what is yours.'*

*26 "But his lord answered and said to him, 'You wicked and lazy servant, you knew that I reap where I have not sown, and gather where I have not scattered seed. 27 So you ought to have deposited my money with the bankers, and at my coming I would have received back my own with interest. 28 So take the talent from him, and give it to him who has ten talents.*

*29 'For to everyone who has, more will be given, and he will have abundance; but from him who does not have, even what he has will be taken away. 30 And cast the unprofitable servant into the outer darkness. There will be weeping and gnashing of teeth."* **Matthew 25:24-30**

Now, I understand that coming right off a chapter on the grace of God, and the freedom in that, this may sound like a heavy downer. Again, we want to use our spiritual maturity here. I would like to reiterate; the difference in the servant in the verses above and the ones preceding him who earned back for their master what they had been given, was a heart condition. In verse 26, the master identifies his heart issues, *"You wicked and lazy servant!"* That's a very scary verse to me. I never, ever want to be guilty of this condition of the heart (look at the consequences in the following verses). Read a little deeper though and see what the servant said. *'And I was afraid, and went and hid your talent in the ground.'* He says he was *afraid.* Consider again the title of this book. God (the Master) saw right through this excuse, and dealt with the core issues.

I know this sounds like a tough way to start a chapter, but please hear where I am coming from. We have an abundance of grace from our heavenly Father, yet He knows our hearts better than we know them ourselves. If you're procrastinating to support Kingdom work, He sees it. If you say you have nothing to give, yet you eat out three or more times a week, He sees it. If you say you can only manage your tithe and you have cable, internet access, Netflix, and the complete package plans for every cell phone in your household, He sees it. I don't say this to condemn anyone, nor make anyone feel guilty, I say it simply to show that we are not to abuse the grace of God, and as we've seen in a previous chapter, we definitely can't claim ignorance. He knows our heart. But again, it's not about a set of rules, the key is bearing fruit. God's kingdom is all about bearing fruit. He expects it of us.

> *'You did not choose Me, but I chose you and appointed you that you should go and bear fruit, and that your fruit should remain, that whatever you ask the Father in My name He may give you.'* **John 15:16**

Each one of us has different fruit we are to bear. Some of us who really have almost nothing financially can volunteer of our time, and talents. So we see regardless of what you *do* or *don't* have, you are still to uphold this mandate of giving. I truly believe that the key to bearing fruit is we are to give as we have the ability to give. Now having said what I wanted to say at the beginning of the chapter, I would like to emphasize the words "ability to give." Some of us have a lot and a lot is expected of us. Just like in the parable of the talents. But, I question whether a lot is expected of those who have been given little. Do you know that there are people going into debt over the fact that they believe they ought to be giving more? They are justifying the fact that they are in debt by giving to Kingdom work, and that surely God will take care of their debt and help them to provide for their needs. This, in my opinion, is bondage. God wants you to be a wise steward. He wants you to bear fruit with what you have, and He'll increase you from there. Going into debt to give is entirely foolish.

Think about fruit. There are already seeds in that fruit. Your spiritual fruit may be physically likened to a watermelon. You can count the seeds in a watermelon, but can you count the watermelons in a seed? If you plant just one seed from your watermelon, how many watermelons could you get back from that seed? This is how God provides. He grows you as you give within your resources, and your ability. God did not expect the lazy servant in the parable above to gain five or even two talents. He said even if the servant had deposited His talent with the bankers, the interest would have gotten him off the hook. God is not unjust. We are to give as we are able.

Now, my ultimate desire in life, and the underlying theme of everything I do in ministry, is to motivate God's people to give to His work. That is ultimately what I believe we need to see happen in Christendom right now, but I don't want to lose sight of the fact that we should not give beyond our financial capacity. I don't believe that God would expect that of us. Our giving has to be according to our financial means. "Now, what about the widow with the two mites?" you might ask. "Surely you're contradicting yourself? She gave *everything*." Indeed. She gave everything, and I believe that is the point Jesus was making. She put her life into God's hands, and Jesus used it as an example that her two mites were worth far more than what the pompous, rich people were giving—because it was everything. Does that mean we are to go and dump our savings, and 401K into the offering on Sunday? No. Start with something small and someday you will grow into the faith this widow had. Give within your ability. Jesus used that widow as an example of a sound heart condition. She would rather have given to God, the little she had to survive another few days, than hoard it. That's a prioritized heart, and I believe Jesus insured she was taken care of for the rest of her life. He did not however, imply that we should all give everything into the offering. Take a look at how the apostle Paul explains this concept:

> '12 For if there is first a willing mind, it is accepted according to what one has, and not according to what he does not have. 13 For I do not mean that others should be eased and you burdened; 14 but by an equality, that now at this time your abundance may supply their lack, that their abundance also may supply your lack—that there may be equality. 15 As it is written, "He who gathered much had nothing left over, and he who gathered little had no lack." ' **2 Corinthians 8:12-15**

Now, I believe that we should always give our tithe to the church, and give sacrificially from time to time. In the chapter this Scripture above is taken from, Paul is giving his church some advice—some things that we, too, should be thinking about in our walk. Things like remembering that God's grace is sufficient at some of our weakest times. Paul is reminding us that we are to continue in the things that we are doing and see them through to completion. Learning this principle is far more important than the quantity of what we give one time, because it will yield more fruit in the long-term. What great advice for us to heed—not to quit or give up on anything, but to continue until we see it to completion, particularly if we believe with our hearts that those desires are from the Lord.

I especially love the reminder in verse 12 that the things that we give are acceptable to God, if it is according to all that we can do. If we have a deep desire to give more, and we give out of all that we have, it is more than acceptable to the Lord. See also the Scripture below where, in Paul's first letter to the Corinthians, he tells them to set aside a sum of money at the beginning of each week (determining in their heart), according to their *income*. This is yet another example, showing that Paul was of the mind that we are only to give according to our means.

> *'1 Now concerning the collection for the*
> *saints, as I have given orders to the churches*
> *of Galatia, so you must do also: 2 On the*
> *first day of the week let each one of you*
> *lay something aside, storing up as he may*
> *prosper, that there be no collections when I*
> *come.'* **1 Corinthians 16:1-2**

I also believe however, that from time to time there may be a check in our spirit to sacrificially give more than what we have been giving regularly, even though it is a little bit of a push, and may seem to be outside of our means. If we are giving a tithe that we feel is a stretch and all that we can give, there may be times when God would challenge us in this, and ask us to give a bit more. He does this because at that point in time, He knows we can. Of course, however, we should always consider prudent and conservative principles for our money management. We cannot give beyond what it is monetarily possible for us to give but if there is room, we should contemplate giving sacrificially.

As I mentioned at the beginning of the chapter, there may be something that we can give up, something unnecessary, something costing us money that we don't even need to be bothered with. If this is the case, then certainly there may be a burden on our heart to give a little bit more (it may even be that God is trying to free us of some hindrance).

In Paul's  second letter to the Corinthians (chapter 8) he says in verses 13 and 14, *'For I do not mean that others should be eased and you burdened; but by an equality, that now at this time your abundance may supply their lack, that their abundance also may supply your lack—that there may be equality.'* Paul is making it clear that if we are lacking in resources it does not mean that we should give beyond what we are able. When we are in abundance and can do so however, we should support, in an abundant way, the work of God, because maybe a brother that has been giving, no longer can.

We ought to evaluate our giving on a regular basis. Is there an element of sacrificial giving? Have we foregone our giving so that we might have something that we do not need? Could we do more for the Kingdom by giving up something that we would like to have? There has to be a balance in our sacrificial giving, for sure, and I do not believe that our giving should be so burdensome that, again, we cannot be a cheerful giver or we give based on unsound financial principles. But, let's stand ready to give sacrificially, as the Lord may ask of us from time to time. He is not going to ask us to do that without a plan to provide for us.

A verse that we would be well-served to remember is Deuteronomy 8:18, where He says, '"And you shall remember the LORD your God, for it is He who gives you power to get wealth, that He may establish His covenant which He swore to your fathers, as it is this day.' The Lord makes it very clear all through Scripture, yet we forget so quickly, that He has established in us the talents, gifts, opportunities, and abilities to generate income—even to create wealth. But we need to remember that it all belongs to the Lord, and it comes from the Lord. He gives the seed to the sower. He gives the increase. So we are to be consistent in our giving, certainly, but we should never be giving beyond our capacity. We need to remember that the Lord has given us what He has given us, and we are to be faithful but wise in this responsibility. That could change—He could give us more, or humble us and give us less for a season. But He will provide, not only for us, but for His Kingdom, so that He may establish it as He swore to the fathers, *"as it is this day"* and I believe it applies to *this* day—*today*.

We are all at different levels of financial independence—some are able to give much financially, some have the ability to give from a smaller portion of finances. Regardless of where you are—from time to time, God will certainly test your faithfulness. If you are faithful, you *will* increase. Please remember, as God multiplies your ability to give financially, it is by Him that these things multiply, and that all that you have is His.

# Chapter Fifteen

# The Reason for Our Giving

*'1 "Take heed that you do not do your charitable deeds before men, to be seen by them. Otherwise you have no reward from your Father in heaven. 2 Therefore, when you do a charitable deed, do not sound a trumpet before you as the hypocrites do in the synagogues and in the streets, that they may have glory from men. Assuredly, I say to you, they have their reward. 3 But when you do a charitable deed, do not let your left hand know what your right hand is doing, 4 that your charitable deed may be in secret; and your Father who sees in secret will Himself reward you openly"'* **Matthew 6:1-4**

I am always amazed at how obvious the opening verses in Matthew 6 are. We see Jesus talking to us about our giving to charity, but especially about giving to please God. When you read that verse, how obvious is it? Of course, we should not be broadcasting all of our good deeds to the whole world. Certainly that would indicate the wrong heart motive to give. Do we need to be cheerfully giving? Yes. Do we need to be freely giving? Absolutely. Should we be giving out of compassion? Without a doubt. Should we be giving for the sense of personal recognition? Well, of course we know the answer to that is *"No."* I believe the only time we should be giving out of a sense of recognition is if that recognition can motivate someone else to give.

If this sounds controversial, allow me to explain beginning with the following Scripture:

> *'7 Did I commit sin in humbling myself that you might be exalted, because I preached the gospel of God to you free of charge? 8 I robbed other churches, taking wages from them to minister to you. 9 And when I was present with you, and in need, I was a burden to no one, for what I lacked the brethren who came from Macedonia supplied. And in everything I kept myself from being burdensome to you, and so I will keep myself. 10 As the truth of*

*Christ is in me, no one shall stop me from this boasting in the regions of Achaia. 11 Why? Because I do not love you? God knows! 12 But what I do, I will also continue to do, that I may cut off the opportunity from those who desire an opportunity to be regarded just as we are in the things of which they boast.'* **2 Corinthians 11:7-12**

This is a very, very interesting passage from the apostle Paul's letter to the Corinthians. Consider what Paul is doing here in light of what Jesus said in Matthew 6. Surely Paul must be sinning, and have his full reward for boasting that he provided for himself, and even boasting about what other churches have given? Not at all. In this example, Paul is doing what he unfortunately had to do his entire ministry— defend his apostleship. It's difficult for us to believe this in retrospect, but at the time Paul was very persecuted, and was treated as a second-class disciple, let alone an apostle, by much of the early church.

But notice something interesting here. Paul is boasting of what other churches have given. He is recognizing what they have given. Ah! So there is something quite amazing. I'm sure the Macedonian brothers didn't support Paul's ministry hoping he would boast of them to the Corinthians (in fact they probably cringed that he used them as an example to chastise the Corinthian church). But after boasting about what the other churches have given, even going so far as to say that he *robbed* the other churches so he wouldn't be a burden to the Corinthians, Paul says he will even boast that he worked to support himself, and took nothing from them. He then explains why in verse 12, *'But what I do, I will also continue to do, that I may cut off the opportunity from those who desire an opportunity to be regarded just as we are in the things of which they boast.'* He is doing this I believe, to not only show the Corinthians the legitimacy of his apostleship, but to spur them on to start giving. I believe he used the phrase *'I robbed other churches, taking wages from them to minister to you.'* very intentionally. He wanted to show them that they weren't even supporting his back-breaking work for the Kingdom, yet they were grumbling and asking if he was even a real apostle.

There were some very evil characters in the early church, just as unfortunately there are today. Paul, using expert wisdom, differentiates between ungodly motivation for recognition, and recognition that is acceptable in God's eyes. Yes, there is a recognition that is acceptable in God's eyes. Notice that Paul was firstly praising the Macedonian brothers for supporting him, and secondly praising other churches for giving what had to be sacrificially to support a church in a different city.

If you're still not convinced, look again at the difference between praising oneself, and someone else praising you. There is recognition in both scenarios, but in the first, there is pride and self-seeking. The difference is in not giving to be recognized, but giving out of love for God. If others commend you for this, then that is one way God is blessing you, but to give hoping to get recognition from others—that too is a trap. Jesus said it this way:

> *'31 "If I bear witness of Myself, My witness is not true. 32 There is another who bears witness of Me, and I know that the witness which He witnesses of Me is true.'* **John 5:31-32**

Consider for example that we often see chapels and buildings on Christian universities named after a particular family. I know many wonder if this is wrong and that we should not be giving with that intent, and for the most part, I certainly agree with that. If however, our giving can be a testimony to someone else, or a motivation to someone else to continue to give for the Kingdom, then I think it's okay if a church or Christian organization boasts of their supporters, just as Paul did. As long as our motivation is not to give to get glory from others, but giving for the glory of God, then those efforts may be an encouragement for other believers to give. Our giving should never be an act of pride or for any other reason than to see the glory of God multiplied and to see the Kingdom of Christ growing. Most of the time giving is done, and should be done, in secret—for the *open* reward that we will receive someday in eternity, and sometimes even here on earth.

Another reason for the naming of a fund or a foundation or a building is that it might help others to see the importance that money can have for the Kingdom of Christ. I know the skeptics will say that it is amazing how a "supposedly" good God can allow so many people in the world to starve. I believe that the goodness of God has given the people of the world enough supply that no one should go hungry. Unfortunately man allowed sin to enter the world, and continues in that sin and greed which now causes the starvation of so many. God has nothing to do with it. People mistake God's eternal sovereignty for an ability to invade our will. I believe this mentality creeps into the church as well, and is a stumbling block even for believers. We put off onto God whatever we find inconvenient, and then expect out of Him whatever we want. But as we saw in the previous chapter, He sees everything we do and knows the detailed motivations of our heart intricately.

I believe another special case is when someone of fame steps up as a spokesperson for the gospel of Jesus Christ, to motivate people to give by their example, and feed the hungry or provide for the poor. In this case, where motivation of others is the true heart intent, I think this leading by example has a far greater impact than if they were to do it in secret. Again, we are to use wisdom in each case. Many of you know John 3:16, but we need to remember 1 John 3:16, as well (and 1 John 3:17 for that matter). John says, *'16 By this we know love, because He laid down His life for us. And we also ought to lay down our lives for the brethren. 17 But whoever has this world's goods, and sees his brother in need, and shuts up his heart from him, how does the love of God abide in him?'*

And on this note, I love 1 John. It is one of my favorite books in the New Testament. John makes a very powerful point about how a person of prominence should lead by example. If we don't share the love of the Lord by sharing the goods and the provisions that He has given us, how can we ever claim the love of God is truly in us? John goes on to say in verse 22 that if we ask of the Lord, He is faithful to give to us, as long as we are doing the things that are pleasing in His sight. I believe giving to the poor is a key to becoming a larger conduit for God's resources (many Scriptures explicitly state this). With all my heart, I believe we ought to be giving from our abundance and that God deeply wants his children to prosper. What father would not want his child to do well, and be able to continue his work in a great way? But, I think some of us forget sometimes that God has prospered us so that we might do a greater good for the Kingdom. This should never be the case. If God has prospered us, or even placed some of us in the limelight, we should lead by example in the limelight. This is not a negative type of recognition. Again, Tim Tebow (Ladies, isn't football great?).

So now I ask, what has God given you, or what has He entrusted to your care? Is it just your finances or your personal goods, or is it simply some of the talents He has given you? Look at what Ezra told the twelve leading priests in Ezra 8:28-29, '*28 And I said to them, "You are holy to the LORD; the articles are holy also; and the silver and the gold are a freewill offering to the LORD God of your fathers. 29 Watch and keep them until you weigh them before the leaders of the priests and the Levites and heads of the fathers' houses of Israel in Jerusalem, in the chambers of the house of the LORD."*'

Ezra was making a very clear point. See, one of the things that we forget about our giving is that like the items in the temple, all of the articles of gold and silver and offerings, everything comes from God, and belongs to God. And that is the truth. Everything we have, we are entrusted with. If you squander the money you have on something inappropriate, you are essentially spending God's resources on that. It puts a whole different perspective on the idea of taking special care of these things. Can you imagine if we looked on all of our possessions that way? We would take on a whole different level of compassion, a whole different level of sincerity. Certainly we would be cheerful in our giving. We would be cheerful in our desires.

We are called not to be lovers of money, so let's use the things that God has entrusted to us—our finances, our personal goods—for the goodness and the glory of God. This is the absolute safest way to approach your finances. I do not believe there has ever been a more urgent time in our nation's history where we need to be raising up children with a biblical world-view. We should be supporting the kinds of education that can incorporate biblical principles into our everyday world. Those things are becoming fewer and farther between, *because there is no support for them.* We need to support the ministries that are proclaiming the gospel of Jesus Christ. We need to support foundations that know what this nation was built upon—the foundation of the Bible. [Again, I ask, are we supporting organizations that are working to restore those foundational cornerstones of America, organizations like American Family Association?] Do you know that there is a Bible buried underneath the Washington Monument, as part of the foundation? What could be a stronger part of the foundation of the Washington Monument? Our forefathers certainly knew that the Bible was the most significant part of our nation, and we need to cause this legacy to thrive again. Can we ever restore that attitude? Not if we don't use the dollars that God has given us to fight.

If we do not rise up in our giving, if we do not understand the simple and basic fundamental principles of stewardship, we are doomed for destruction. This begins with the correct motivation. We have seen the deterioration of the moral fiber of this country, and the increase of greed and corruption. We, as believers, need to finance the things that are going to bring this country not only to its knees (in prayer), but make this country great. These are the things of the Lord. We cannot do this with an incorrect motivation. A soon as we seek recognition for our giving, the reason for our giving is tarnished, and we fall under the influence of our enemy. The same enemy that is trying to hijack this country and the Church. Right now, we can expect that the government is not going to support the biblical beliefs that we know are true. We can be sure that the secular world, the non-believers, are not going to support the proclamation of the gospel, nor are they going to support the revival that is needed in this country and throughout the world. *We* have to do it, and we cannot be spiritually sabotaged in this great work by being tempted to give for the wrong reasons.

It is essential that we understand the importance of giving to Church and ministries that are directly or indirectly proclaiming the gospel. Ezra certainly knew that all the articles and all the possessions in the temple belonged to God. We need to know that all that we have, whether it's our talents, our abilities, our time, or the opportunities we have been given—they all came from God, and ultimately belong to God. We need to make the best of them to honor and glorify Him in secret, so He can multiply us as He sees fit. When our harvest is multiplied and increased, we need to seek and save the lost, and continually support the biblical world-view that will set us apart as a people, and a nation, and hopefully set the world apart for the purposes and glory of God. How will this be accomplished if we do not learn the basics of giving for the right reason, and then graduate to giving to those things that promote biblical literacy, a biblical world-view, and the ministries proclaiming God's Word? I believe we can be joyful celebrators with God in His work as we give with a willing heart, for His purposes.

# Chapter Sixteen

# Involving God in Every Aspect of Our Lives

As this book draws to a close, I would like to recap what we've been talking about, and add a few more thoughts in regard to the broader picture. It is evident that many of us live in a fear of money. This is highly contradictory to God's nature because the writer of Hebrews says, *'But without faith it is impossible to please Him, for he who comes to God must believe that He is, and that He is a rewarder of those who diligently seek Him'* **(Heb. 11:6).** So living in fear actually displeases God.

We also saw that money is simply a symbol, or a token of the real sweat and labor we perform every day. It is a very crude, primitive way to measure our labor, and the love and worship of this symbol, money, is one of the reasons the world is so corrupt. Unfortunately, it is what it is, and will continue so this side of Heaven. The upside is that money, when used wisely, can be a magnificent tool to spread the gospel, in the hands of believers. The point here however, is that if we say we have given our lives to God, but are not free with our money, we are not speaking the truth.

I don't want you to get into condemnation however. There is a method to becoming free of the fear of money, and in the next chapter I will briefly outline some practical steps to work toward this goal. The secret is, just like with salvation, allowing God to work on your heart. If you change your heart simply to a state where it is open to obedience to the Holy Spirit, half the battle is won. The other half is remaining consistent, and vigilant in your daily effort to keep your heart in the right place, and hear His voice. I believe, actually that's not right—I *know* He has a very specific plan for you, but it's only through relationship with Him that you will ever fulfill this plan.

Sadly many, many Christians barely even start walking out God's plan for them, simply because they are content to go through the motions and never really build a deep relationship with Jesus. Unfortunately we are living in crazy times, and it is no longer a world in which we can glide by in our little comfort bubble. I believe the faith of Christians is about to be tested in a very real way throughout the world. Just look at world events, even the natural disasters that are taking place on an unprecedented level. Things are being shaken up, but again, we are not to live in fear. God will take care of us, but it is only through consistent, daily relationship with Him that He can actually accomplish this fully.

This is why as the head of a "financial ministry" I wanted to write a book that will highlight two critical ideas. If you take nothing away from this book except these two ideas, I will feel as though I have accomplished what the Lord asked me to. First, we are to have a change of heart. A change of heart regarding our priorities, our money, and our relationship with God. Jesus is the true Treasure and in Him, everything we need is found. Please, fellow believers, understand this isn't merely a Christian sentiment, or cliché to be repeated with lots of other Christian jargon on Sunday mornings. *This is (hopefully) a life-changing concept.* You must break up the fallow ground of your heart, as God instructed through the prophet Hosea. We are to repent, yes, repent of our fear, lack of trust and hoarding and spend time learning to hear the voice of God through Scripture, and in our heart, based on Scripture. I cannot emphasize this enough.

Secondly, we are to support and fund expansion of the Kingdom of God. Without our hearts being fully submitted to God, and the fear of money removed, this cannot happen on the scale that is necessary to get our nation, and the world out of the hellish condition we are already in, and is about to get worse. Only the gospel of Jesus Christ can rescue this world from the brink of disaster. The first step is to get your heart in the right place. Plan for your family's financial well-being. That is scriptural, and in fact a commandment. (1 Tim. 5:8) Do this, but keep your focus also on supporting Kingdom expansion. Make giving to the work of God your priority. As a layperson, not in full-time ministry, supporting sound, effective ministries is paramount to your calling, and continued fruit-bearing.

The focus of this book is defeating the fear of money, but since the expansion of the Kingdom of God is the true focus, I will mention here that money is not the only way you can support the Kingdom. Not that this is to be used as a cop-out. If you have skills and talents, or even if you don't, you should be volunteering time in your local church and seeing if there is anything extra you can do for evangelistic ministries God has placed on your heart. You should also however, be trusting God with you money, and be giving financially to support the work of God.

So we see that when we get our heart in the right place, submit to God and trust Him, we have actually just begun on the path toward fulfilling His goals for our life. Towards the end of his life, the apostle Paul says to his disciple Timothy, *'7 I have fought the good fight, I have finished the race, I have kept the faith. 8 Finally, there is laid up for me the crown of righteousness, which the Lord, the righteous Judge, will give to me on that Day, and not to me only but also to all who have loved His appearing'* **(2 Tim. 4:7-8).** Paul successfully completed his mission for God. This took years, and years of consistent obedience and relationship with God, but look at what Paul accomplished! Imagine what you can accomplish when you make a decision to stop living in fear, and instead live by faith! Paul is also encouraging Timothy here to do the same, and what he is really saying is, *"Put in the consistent effort, because before you've even noticed the sacrifice, you'll have the reward!"*

There is nothing greater that you can spend your life on than being a part of spreading the gospel of Jesus Christ. You can do this not only with your money, but in every area of your daily life. At work, not Bible-bashing, or weaving in a Scripture with every sentence you speak to your unbelieving coworkers, but with your example. Your love. Your kindness. Your generosity. When you are spending time with God in prayer, and reading His Word consistently, His love and nature will shine through you. It will be effortless. Jesus said His burden was light, and He was meek and humble, so we should follow Him. It is not difficult, it just requires a soft, pliable heart.

We examined the law of sowing and reaping as well. When you are supporting God's Kingdom, do you think He's going to let a skilled, faithful soldier in His army (that's you!) lack any resources? Of course not! Jesus said this in Mark's gospel:

> *'28 Then Peter began to say to Him, "See, we have left all and followed You." 29 So Jesus answered and said, "Assuredly, I say to you, there is no one who has left house or brothers or sisters or father or mother or wife or children or lands, for My sake and the gospel's, 30 who shall not receive a hundredfold now in this time—houses and brothers and sisters and mothers and children and lands, with persecutions— and in the age to come, eternal life.'*
> **Mark 10:28-30**

Jesus promised us a hundred times more in this present age! Remember the parable of the sower? The degrees of reward for those whose hearts are good ground? Some thirty, some sixty, and some a hundred fold. Jesus was saying if you're truly submitted to Him, and are willing to do anything He asks, you will receive a hundred times more, even in this life. That's not a prosperity gospel, that's Jesus saying you will have anything and everything you need! The genius of God's ways of course, is His reward is based on the motivation of your heart. As soon as you give with the motivation of greed, or recognition, you hinder this spiritual law.

We saw this in the contrast Jesus exposes between the widow with her two mites and the rich leaders in Mark 12. The widow's heart was right, so her two pennies were worth more than all of the gold and silver the arrogant rich were throwing in the treasury. They were giving for recognition. She was giving out of sacrificial love.

Now as I explained, we are not under any legal obligation to give. This actually becomes a non-issue when our hearts are submitted to God, and taking direction from the Holy Spirit. In this scenario, the Holy Spirit guides us in what we should be giving, and we can hear Him clearly, because of our diligent relationship with Him. A wonderful example of the freedom and provision God counters condemnation with is found in Matthew 17:

> *'24 When they had come to Capernaum, those who received the temple tax came to Peter and said, "Does your Teacher not pay the temple tax?" 25 He said, "Yes." And when he had come into the house, Jesus anticipated him, saying, "What do you think,*

*Simon? From whom do the kings of the earth take customs or taxes, from their sons or from strangers?" 26 Peter said to Him, "From strangers." Jesus said to him, "Then the sons are free. 27 Nevertheless, lest we offend them, go to the sea, cast in a hook, and take the fish that comes up first. And when you have opened its mouth, you will find a piece of money; take that and give it to them for Me and you."'* **Matthew 17:24-27**

I love this so much. These tax collectors were not just trying to innocently collect the tax. They asked, *'Does your Teacher not pay the temple tax?"'* They were trying to subversively accuse and condemn Jesus, and His disciples. You will always, always, always encounter persecution when you start serving the Lord. As we saw in the above Scripture in Mark 10, when Jesus told us we'd receive a hundred-fold return for wholly following Him, He guaranteed persecution with it.

Jesus answers with such amazing wisdom as always. He asks Peter a very important question. Are they not required to pay the temple tax, since they are sons of the Kingdom, and the temple really belongs to God? What Jesus is saying here is they are actually exempt, not because God shows favoritism, but rather that word *sons* has connotations that lean more towards *civil servants*. They are in the service of the temple, so why should they pay to perform their own duties? Jesus answers the legalism and then watch how He handles the tax collectors. He demonstrates His love, authority, royalty, and absolute power in this one little incident. He doesn't want to offend the tax collectors, even though they are trying to accuse Him! He still cares about their eternal life. Even though they are truly His enemies, He still cares for them and doesn't want to offend them so some day, they may have a hope of entering His Kingdom, too. Next, He doesn't pay the tax out of His ministry's account. Oh no, He's way too cool for that. He tells Peter to catch a fish, and pay them with the coin that he will find in the fish's mouth. Wow! Jesus demonstrates several things here. First, He is not subject to this world's primitive system because He is the Son of the true Kingdom. He performs a miracle to show that He is not a tax evader, and not only has the money, He can answer their petty accusations with a payment out of seemingly thin air. This demonstrates His power, royalty, and authority. What stands out most for me is found in verse 27: *'take that and give it to them for Me and you.'* My tax and yours! This demonstrates Jesus provides for *both* Peter and Himself. He does the same for us. We are sons and daughters of the Kingdom—if we are free of the fear of money, He will get the resources out of a fish's mouth if He wants to make a point!

The nugget of truth here, to recap, is that we are to never give under compulsion. In my opinion, we are legally not required to give any specific amount. What we are required to give is our heart, which would be a willingness to give everything if He asked for it. When He has that level of submission, the point of a legal requirement to give becomes a non-issue because we understand that it is all His anyway.

Lastly, we see that our motivation for giving must never, ever be out of a desire for recognition. This will sabotage and foul up everything. Here's why: 1) Our heart is in the wrong place. God can't work with it to truly do what He needs to do with us, and His plan for our lives and spiritual growth; 2) It is a terrible example for weaker believers. If they see wrong motivations being flaunted, they could either be disgusted and turn away from the faith, or emulate it; 3) If we give out of a wrong motivation, we probably won't be giving where God needs us to, because we aren't in relationship with Him.

Now good motivation is when mature, sincere believers recognize another for their giving effort. We can commend sincere people, who are humble enough to not even desire the recognition, but instead just want to further the Kingdom of God. It is somewhat ironic that this is the case, but we saw Paul commend the Galatian church for their gifts, and a group of Macedonian believers for supporting Paul in ministering to the Corinthian church.

So here's a 30,000 foot view of what we need to do to be free of the fear of money. We have to start by repenting for our fear (lack of trust), and disobedience in our finances. God is faithful and just to forgive us. (**1 John 1:9**) He's our Father, He just wants us to grow. This puts our heart on the correct starting blocks. Next, we need to develop our relationship with Him through prayer and our knowledge of Scripture. We need to study the Bible, and read commentaries, and get rid of the intimidation of theology, and just read the Word as a practical letter to us. The best way to understand the Bible is by spending some time in prayer before reading it. When we pray, we align our spirit with the Holy Spirit, and He can then enlighten us in regard to the Scriptures. You will be blown away at how this works. Try it, and see. Pray for fifteen minutes or so, and then read a passage of Scripture. You'll see the meaning in that Scripture as you've never seen before. This is a huge part of your relationship with God. The apostle John calls Jesus the Word. The Bible is essentially the nature of Jesus Christ revealed. If you want to understand and know Jesus, He's revealed in the Word.

Lastly, be consistent. Everyone can start out well, but it's those who finish well, just like Paul, that receive the big prizes. The key to being consistent is relationship. I may sound like a cracked record, but this level of relationship is deeper than just prayer and Bible study. It's a worship of God. An intimate love for Him that you express in your prayer time but can also be expressed throughout the day. Let your thoughts just fill with His wonder and beauty throughout your day. This will energize you, and strengthen you. Look at the sun outside, at the trees, listen to the birds and just take in all that He has created for you! He didn't have to make it so beautiful. He did it as a husband would make the most beautiful valentine for his darling wife. He created this beautiful planet you call home, to show you how much He loves you! Think about that, and thank Him for it. This will bring you joy, and the joy of the Lord will be your strength. **(Neh. 98:10)**

In the next chapter, I will give a more detailed view of practical steps you can take, based on the book, so that you can free yourself of the fear of money, and begin to thrive in what God has called you to in supporting the Kingdom.

# Chapter Seventeen

# A Practical Summary

Books that have only theory are only half useful in my opinion. In this chapter, I wanted to provide a summary of the practical steps you can take to begin implementing the principles found in this book. This is a very high overview of course, but could act as an in-depth step-by-step guide to building faith in God into your life, and edging the fear of money out. Use this chapter in your small group study.

**Understand and acknowledge how we compartmentalize our money away from God**

Worry, procrastination, and disobedience. These are the key elements that cause us to compartmentalize our money away from God. The real killer here is when we won't acknowledge what we are doing. Hopefully, the first chapter of this book shed some light on how and why this happens, and you've been liberated from this way of thinking. It doesn't matter what's in the past, even what causes us to separate our faith from our finances, the most important thing to do first is to acknowledge we do it.

A good way to acknowledge it is to take a look at our finances and try to figure up a percentage of what we give to the work of God. Average everything you've given from helping any Christian non-profit, and then see what percentage that is of your total income. Now look at what you've spent your money on (maybe you are using some software, like Quicken Home). If you don't have records of this data, track your spending, income, and giving over the next month, and that will give you a snapshot. I expect it will be quite sobering to see how much of a priority you've made Kingdom expansion. Don't worry though, there is no condemnation, just get serious about changing, and learning how. The fact that you've read this book speaks volumes.

**Understand why Jesus is the real Treasure**

Read chapter three of this book, and study the names of God. Meditate on them. Search them out in Scripture. Read commentaries on them. This will begin to give you a deeper knowledge of who Jesus Christ really is.

When you have studied the names of God a little, you will begin to understand that your complete provision is in Him. This is very good news for your soul. Once you have studied His names, or in tandem with that study, begin reading the book of John. John's writing is wonderful, and requires a little knowledge of the foreshadowing of Christ in the Old Testament, but John's love for the Master shines through. Hopefully, this will rub off on you.

Remember the pearl merchant who sold everything he had to buy the one, rare Pearl he had. He could only do that by searching and searching. Seek Jesus in the same way. Strive to know Him and build a relationship with Him. You will find He is already knocking on the door of your heart. Once you begin to know Him, your entire perspective will shift. You will see how money is just a means to an end—sharing Jesus with this whole world. If the entire world had a revelation of who Jesus Christ really is, how gentle, how powerful, how absolutely loving He is, all our problems would be over tomorrow. He is the best gift you can give, and the greatest security you can ever have. When you build a deeper relationship with Him you'll understand why. Then your fear of money, the tight grip you have on it—and it has on you—will quickly begin to evaporate.

## Repent

This is almost a dirty word in today's self-entitled, prideful world. It's also one of the most powerful ways to instantly gain the favor of God. James says, *"But he gives us more grace. That is why Scripture says: 'God opposes the proud but shows favor to the humble'"* (James 4:6). When you acknowledge that you have been compartmentalizing a large part of your life away from God, but claiming to have given your life to Him, your heart is softening. When you realize that you cannot continue like this, and truly apologize to God for your error and arrogance, His hand of favor will quickly turn to you.

Be real with Him. He knows it's not easy to rid yourself of fear after operating in it for so many years. But repent of it. Repent means "turn away" in the Hebrew. Turn away from your fear, and trust Him. The only way to do this is to remain in relationship with Him. Get down on your knees and cry before Him like David did in Psalm 119:169: *'Let my cry come before You, O LORD; Give me understanding according to Your word.'*

Repent and commit to the following action items:

## Spend time in prayer

Starting today, not tomorrow morning, spend at least twenty minutes a day in prayer. Prayer is a fancy word for "hanging out with God." Don't over religious-ize prayer. Speak to God as you would a friend. He loves you, and knows your heart. When you pray like this, it isn't a burden, it's full of enjoyment. We were built for relationship. If you are doing it right, prayer will be something you look forward to every day. Remember it's about getting to know Him. There is a reverence that needs to be present (He is God, after all), but be honest with Him. And always be in recognition and acknowledge that His name is Hallowed and He is the Lord of your life.

Speak to Him about everything you're going through, and make your requests to Him, but also be sure to tell Him how much you appreciate His love and grace. We are made in His image, so this shouldn't be hard to imagine. He loves it when His children notice what He does for them, just as you do when your children hug you and say they love you. He does so much for us. Thank Him, and also worship Him as God. Worship Him. He's gentle, and kind and loving. He's also all-powerful.

Lastly, speak to Him but spend time listening as well. This is extremely important. So many people go to pray and just rattle off a laundry list of requests to God, run out of things to ask for and then think they've spent time with Him. How would you like to spend time with someone like that? No, listen to Him. Sometimes He'll speak directly to your heart, and just "show" you things in your heart. You'll just understand something new, or a certain path you need to take, but you will know it's God's leading. Believe He hears you when you pray and then listen for His voice. Often it is a small still voice, you may not hear it in the middle of your talking, still yourself. You will jump for joy the first time you know that you know He's spoken to you. One of the clearest ways He'll speak to you as well is He'll show you specific things for your life out of the Word.

**Read your Bible with purpose and intent**

> *'The grass withers, the flower fades, But*
> *the word of our God stands forever."*
> **Isaiah 40:8**

The Bible is the Word of God. Whether secular pundits agree or not, means nothing. The resurrection of Jesus Christ is proof that He is the Son of God, just as He said and that He is alive and well today in His resurrected body. The resurrection has been proven by many facts that history has simply no other explanation for. If historians (or scientists) can be trusted regarding any of their assertions, the resurrection has to be at the forefront of the pack with sound evidence. (Read Josh McDowell's *The Resurrection Factor* for a fascinating insight into how undeniable the resurrection is.)

If the resurrection is true, it is pretty safe to assume Jesus must be who He said He is. The Son of God. Jesus relied on Scripture as the inspired Word of God. This means you should, too. These simple facts have staggering implications. Jesus made some mind-boggling statements regarding Himself and the authority He delegated to us. Basically, He gave us back complete dominion over this world (Adam lost it in the garden through sin). The Bible is a legal document of your rights, as a son or daughter of the Kingdom of the Living God. Paul calls us *joint heirs* with Christ so we know this is true. Here's a startling fact however; many Christians will live their entire life without even scratching the surface of appropriating what *legally* belongs to them. Satan robs us by fear, complacency, and pride. Reading the Bible is the antidote to such ignorance.

You've heard the term "knowledge is power"? Hosea 4:6 says, *'My people are destroyed for lack of knowledge....'* It can literally be lethal to not know the Word of God. Thank God, He protects us however, and guards us until He can lead us into growing into His Word.

Start reading the gospel of John as I mentioned earlier in this chapter. Assign at least twenty minutes to an hour each day. There is nothing more important in your schedule than this and prayer. While you're reading, read a corresponding commentary to gain new insights, and truly understand some scriptural background to what you're reading. Most smartphones have free Bible apps with commentaries in them. I like Pocketsword right now.

Also, ask your Sunday school teacher. Join a home group. Ask questions. Read the study material. Find a church where you can get spiritually fulfilled each week, where you will leave each Sunday and hopefully Wednesday night closer to God than you were last week. Soak up as much knowledge about the Bible as possible and as you hear it go home and check it out. I know he's the Pastor but a good pastor would want you to do that. Believe me—it will amaze you how little you really know and how much you will grow. I'm in the same boat but blessed to sit each week—twice some weeks—under an incredibly gifted Pastor and teacher, (you can listen to his verse by verse of John as you read it at www.cc-chestersprings.com).

So get to know the Word. Understand who Jesus really is. When you begin to get the Word into your spirit, and couple this with prayer, I *guarantee* your life will change. If you do this consistently for three months, you'll be a completely changed person, free of fear, and living for the eternal Kingdom of God! Learn as a good student so you'll be ready when you're elevated to a high rank in God's kingdom. Also, if this is all new to you check out www.knowhim.afr.net

## Expect your seed to be multiplied

We've seen in Hebrews 11:6, the writer says, *'But without faith it is impossible to please Him, for he who comes to God must believe that He is, and that He is a rewarder of those who diligently seek Him.'* The reason God wants us to have faith is that it is like spiritual *currency*! Faith moves God. This is how God operates. He expects a return on His seed. First, you have to believe that God exists, but you have to also believe He is going to bless you when you earnestly seek Him! This ties in to the Pearl of great price, doesn't it? We have to expect God to bless us. He gives seed to the sower, so take Him at His word and expect that He is just going to give you your seed. Have faith!

So live in expectation that God is going to lead you into blessings, so you can be a blessing to others. Watch out for good opportunities. When an opportunity arises, always pray about it. Pray until you know in your knower, that you have an answer. It will feel "right" when it's of God. It will feel "anxious" or uneasy or unsure when it's not. Sometimes it's half right but you have to pray through seeking exactly how to move ahead. I still struggle with discernment but I have gotten better. You will too if you keep at it.

Isaiah 55:11 says, *'So shall My word be that goes forth from My mouth; It shall not return to Me void, But it shall accomplish what I please, And it shall prosper in the thing for which I sent it.'* God expects a return on His investment. He doesn't invest foolishly. You should do the same. In fact, since I just quoted that Scripture, Proverbs 18:21 says, *'Death and life are in the power of the tongue, And those who love it will eat its fruit.'* One of the most powerful things you can do is speak the Word of God over your finances, or any situation in your life. Find applicable Scriptures (there are several websites where you can search-by-topic and find Scripture relating to what you need). Pray these Scriptures over your situation. In fact, these Scriptures are your legal document, more iron-clad than any security in this world. For example, Philippians 4:19 says, *'And my God shall supply all your need according to His riches in glory by Christ Jesus.'* This is literally a Scripture you can take to the bank! Is this a prosperity gospel? No, *"God shall supply all your need"* The emphasis is on needs! With that we are content, but when you have your priorities in line, expect God to bless you as a faithful servant. Just don't rely on or focus on the blessing. Expect your seed to be multiplied so you can do more for the Kingdom!

## If you have been blessed with wealth, ask God how to best use it

Basically, you have to surrender it to Him. Just like the rich man who built a bigger barn to hoard when God blessed Him, you can learn the hard way that it belongs to God anyway, or you can learn the easy way and submit it to Him. This is an infinitely more secure way to live in the long run. Submit your wealth to God. Again, I'm not saying you should give it all away. No, develop your prayer life, knowledge of the Word, and relationship with Him and you'll begin to sense for what, how, and where He wants you to use your resources.

The apostle Paul instructs his disciple Timothy concerning wealthy church members. Timothy at this point, was leading a very large church, as a relatively young man. Look at what Paul says:

> '17 Command those who are rich in this present age not to be haughty, nor to trust in uncertain riches but in the living God, who gives us richly all things to enjoy. 18 Let them do good, that they be rich in good works, ready to give, willing to share, 19 storing up for themselves a good foundation for the time to come, that they may lay hold on eternal life.' **1 Timothy 6:17-19**

It's pretty clear here what the Holy Spirit is saying through the apostle Paul. Do good, and in fact be rich in good deeds. This is far more rewarding to the soul, even in this life. Put your hope in God. This is the key. You will never be able to hang on to enough of your money. Give it to God, (spiritually) and He will do amazing things with it. Lay up treasure for yourself as a firm foundation in the coming age (Heaven), so that you may take hold of that which is truly life. The good life! Commit your finances to God, and do good works. You'll never regret it. Keep in mind as a resource American Family Association 800-326-4543 X 206 or 233. They will, for free, give you trusted guidance through your planning if you want to include God's Ministries with a portion of your blessings.

### Start small but become consistent

This is really as simple as it sounds so I won't spend a ton of time on this section. I almost titled this section "If you have little, start small but become consistent" but I realized it's true of any station in life. Start small and grow your faith. But as you should be consistent in your growth in faith, be consistent also in your giving. Don't promise God an impossibility; the harvest will come as you plant with faith not because of what you want from the harvest but because of what you know God can do with it.

*'26 And He said, "The kingdom of God is as if a man should scatter seed on the ground, 27 and should sleep by night and rise by day, and the seed should sprout and grow, he himself does not know how. 28 For the earth yields crops by itself: first the blade, then the head, after that the full grain in the head. 29 But when the grain ripens, immediately he puts in the sickle, because the harvest has come."'* **Mark 4:26-29**

The Lord is actually saying two things here. First, He is saying, simply plant your seed by putting in the effort in the right places and it grows. You don't even know how, but it grows! This is a very reassuring Scripture. Second, the Lord is saying that it grows in stages. Your faith, and your relationship with Him is the same way. Don't expect God to give you a million dollars, when your need is only a hundred. First, give the homeless man a sandwich, and trust God to give you money to continue to do His work on the street, and share the love of Christ. When He provides that sandwich, trust Him for a soup kitchen. When He provides that, who knows what's next? Grow in stages, and enjoy every minute of it.

I want to emphasize here as well to begin within your means, as you are able. Again, the key is to follow the leading of the Holy Spirit through prayer and Bible study, and then use wisdom. There is much wisdom in common sense. God will not guide with the outlying stuff, that deviates from the norm of natural sense. Don't go looking for the "mystical" or the "spooky," wanting to give everything away and "trusting" God for a million dollars for no good reason. Use wisdom. Determine to begin giving a certain amount consistently. Then trust God to provide more seed for you to sow. In the course of time, you can give sacrificially every so often, and leap up to the next level.

**Watch out for legalism**

The only way to effectively avoid legalism is to continuously remain in relationship with the Lord. Legalism creeps in when you neglect this and try to "shortcut" a real relationship with God by trying to substitute a lot of laws or totally relying on the non-biblical mandates of a pastor. As we've seen in all denominations and churches, this can and will happen. Just stay in relationship with Him, in His word and He'll guide you perfectly in and out of every day, and situation. When your heart is right, and you're being led by the Lord, you'll never have to worry how much to give, or when to give or what ministry to give to. You'll just know it, because He'll tell you in your spirit. This concept is explained again by Paul in his letter to the Romans. I believe Romans chapter 8 is one of the deeper chapters in the Word:

> *'1 There is therefore now no condemnation to those who are in Christ Jesus, who do not walk according to the flesh, but according to the Spirit. 2 For the law of the Spirit of life in Christ Jesus has made me free from the law of sin and death. 3 For what the law could not do in that it was weak through the flesh, God did by sending His own Son in the likeness of sinful flesh, on account of sin: He condemned sin in the flesh, 4 that the righteous requirement of the law might be fulfilled in us who do not walk according to the flesh but according to the Spirit.'*
> **Romans 8:1-4**

I explained the middle verses in chapter 13, but don't worry too much about those verses right now. Focus first on verse 1, *'There is therefore now no condemnation to those who are in Christ Jesus.'* This proves what I just explained. If you remain *in* Christ Jesus, living in Him, in relationship with Him, there is no condemnation. He freed us from the sin condemnation that the law can bring. In fact, the Holy

Spirit will fulfill the law through you, when you are being led by Him.

Second, look at the last half of verse 3, and verse 4. '...*He condemned sin in the flesh, 4 that the righteous requirement of the law might be fulfilled in us who do not walk according to the flesh but according to the Spirit.*' The *righteous* requirement of the law will be *fully* met in us because we don't live according to our fleshly desires (like hoarding money) but according to the Spirit. This is the way to remain free of legalism. Live according to the Word.

When we're too lazy to seek God's specific will, we are in danger of falling into routine and legalism. If you ever feel compelled to give, or burdened, check your prayer life, and Bible reading, and ask yourself what is going on? Are you hearing from God or just being lazy and giving a certain amount to cover a requirement. Never neglect your Bible reading, prayer time, and relationship with God and you won't fall victim to condemnation.

## Sacrificial giving

When you're practicing the steps above begin to look for how you might give sacrificially to the Kingdom. In fact, by the time you're praying consistently and reading the Word, the Holy Spirit will have probably begun to give you insight and wisdom into managing your finances, and other areas of your life. All of this blossoms out of a relationship with Him in beautiful synergy.

If you're still not sure just ask yourself what frivolous things you pay for or own that you don't need? Is there even anything just sitting around your house that you know someone else in your church, or a neighbor could use? Take the opportunity to share the love of Christ maybe, or just help someone in need.

Beyond that, be sure to consider what you can give over and above your current, consistent giving. If you are truly just making ends meet, can you sacrifice eating out one time and giving the money to the Lord? Can you choose a gym that is cheaper, shower at home and give the extra to the Lord each month? There is great reward in this sort of giving. There is a secret not many people know about the sacrifices in the Old Testament. God required the first-born of all animals, the first of the harvest, even the firstborn child was automatically dedicated as holy to the Lord. (**Exod. 13:2**) God required the firstborn for several reasons but one of them is that the firstborn is very valuable. Especially in humans, the firstborn child is a very special, momentous birth. Each child is celebrated but every parent will tell you, when you're green and don't know what you're doing, that child's birth and first few months are embedded in your memory forever.

In the same way, when we give something valuable it is extremely precious in the Lord's sight. As an aside, that is why timing is important to Him, too. Don't wait two weeks to give your offering. As soon as you get that deposit, be ready with your check for the offering and be happy you can give back to the Lord for how He's blessing you! Don't deny yourself that wonderful act of worship.

### Keep a daily (yes daily) motivation check

As you grow in your gift of faith, and your mustard seed becomes a tall tree bearing fruit, and bringing shade, and nesting birds, Satan will use a new, sneaky tactic to try to trip you up. Pride. Always make sure you're giving without the desire for recognition, even secretly if you must, so you will never fall prey to this subtle but lethal attack.

In your prayer time every day, pray the Lord keeps you humble and focused on His work and His Kingdom. When you're faithful, God will bless you. That is an absolute, spiritual law. You can't get around it even if you wanted to. As you give more and more, and God honors you and grows you, don't be like Solomon (Eccles.) and begin to believe it is your own wisdom that accomplished your blessings. Nothing disappoints God quicker.

Commit your heart to follow this truth: If God *never* brings you recognition for you giving, but only reveals your years of silent service in Heaven, let that be enough for you. The best way to insure this is in the next section.

## Become Heavenly Minded

When you're practicing all of these principles successfully for a length of time, you're going to see some real progress in your spiritual walk. You probably will hardly be able to believe how far you've come from being in the bondage of fear of money, to living by faith in total freedom. If you're truly reading the Word, praying and studying, the Holy Spirit will be giving you revelations of His Kingdom, and how it works. This is called becoming "Heavenly minded." The Kingdom of Heaven isn't just for "up there" and "someday."

Start by building up your local church. In fact, to do that you need to find a good, solid church that teaches the Word of God in sound, stable doctrine. Don't church hop. No church is perfect, and if it was it would become imperfect as soon as you and I walked through the door, so find a good church—one where the Gospel is being proclaimed, where you are being spiritually fed and where you are seeing people come to Christ. Begin connecting and serving there, and support your local church with your giving, then find some evangelistic ministries and missions-based ministries to give to. Remember, it's up to God's people to financially insure our church doors stay open.

When you begin to see life in the context of eternity, you really do realize it is only a breath. The apostle James says, *'whereas you do not know what will happen tomorrow. For what is your life? It is even a vapor that appears for a little time and then vanishes away'* (James 4:14). This is so true. For you young people, in two blinks you will be of retirement age, looking back on what you've done with your life. Be Heavenly minded and you'll accomplish the most value with your life. Give it to God, and He'll work wonders with your life. The key is to live in light of eternity, and to focus on spreading the most important message on the planet—the gospel of Jesus Christ.

> *'The plans of the diligent lead surely to plenty, But those of everyone who is hasty, surely to poverty.'* **Proverbs 21:5**

The Scripture above is truly faithful to keep you safe and sound in any financial crisis, chaos, or general financial fear. Diligently practice what you have learned in this book and you will absolutely be free of the fear of money, and instead be a victorious, abundantly provisioned soldier of Christ. It takes diligence. Just like any skill or conditioning, you need to begin with a little and build your strength. The beauty of following these steps is not only will you have peace about your financial life, God will change every aspect of your life as you diligently deepen your relationship with Him.

# Chapter Eighteen

# Conclusion

In conclusion, I wanted to pass along a personal message, from my heart. We cannot truly say we love the Lord and give glory to Him in all we do, while we compartmentalize any segment of our lives away from His counsel and direction. It all has to be recognized—that the good in our lives, both the opportunities and our abilities, come from God. We need to fall on our knees each and every day, as we give our fears over to the Lord and give him gratitude for what we have.

You can imagine that in over fifteen years on the radio I have heard many comments from people about their finances. I have too often heard people moaning and complaining about their circumstances, while they have a car to drive, a roof over their head, their health, and a job. There is not much more that matters than that, yet it is so easy to fall into the deception of riches. If you think you aren't rich consider that if you live on more than $10 a day, you are in the elite top 20 percent of human beings living on this planet. In our post-modern, materialistic societies, we can easily forget our blessings, and this is a trap. That is why I know without a doubt, that this world is corrupt and thank God, temporary, and the only worthwhile pursuit is a deep, sacrificial love for our Lord and Savior, who leads by example. I pray if nothing else, these sentiments in the book have touched your heart.

If you read this book and you do not have a personal relationship with Jesus Christ, please know this: He is ready for you to come to Him today. It doesn't matter what fears or anxieties you have. It doesn't matter where you have been or where you have dreamed of going. Jesus doesn't care about the sins of your past. He only cares about His fellowship with you in the future. He loves you personally, passionately, and more than you can fathom. Of that I am absolutely certain.

Struggle as you might to get rid of the fears and anxieties of your circumstances or finances, it is impossible to gain victory in that area without the knowledge and the saving grace of Jesus Christ. Take it from someone who can say that I was the wretch whom the song ("Amazing Grace") was talking about. I too came to Christ later in my life at a time when I thought I certainly could not even begin to be worthy of God's grace. How wrong I was about that, and how wrong you are if you are also thinking that. God knows your heart. If you desire to begin a relationship with Him, and if you desire to put your fears aside and give them over to Christ, it does not matter how you word it. The only thing that matters is the attitude of your heart, as you submit your life to Him, in exchange for infinitely more. This exchange is even better than compound interest!

You can pray to receive Christ even now. Don't come to the table of God because of what He is serving, but rather to discover Him. Because relationship is what is void in your life and heart, He is the ultimate remedy.

I would suggest a prayer like this:

> *Lord Jesus, I want to know You personally. Thank You for dying on the cross for my sins. I now open the door of my life and I receive You as my Lord and Savior.*
>
> *Thank You for forgiving me of my sins, and giving me eternal life and eternal fellowship with You. Please take control of my life and make me the kind of person You want me to be. Amen*

A simple prayer like that, with a heart attitude that is right, will soon make your concerns about the "lack of, or too much" money secondary. Perhaps you need to recommit your life today. If that is the case, I hope that you will pray a similar prayer. I hope you will find a great church that will feed you with sound doctrine and draw you closer to Him. Just remain in daily relationship with Him, and you'll stay on track, and grow.

Thank you for the time you took to read this book and thank you for your prayers for our ministry. I pray that God richly blesses you in the life-changing knowledge of Jesus Christ. Always remember that all that you are and all you have is HIS. I'm confident you'll be found to be a faithful steward—God has saved us so that we might reflect Him in our work, ways, words and walk. We are the body of Christ. God bless you.

**Intermedia Publishing Group**

*Publishing That Works For You*

**Do you need a speaker?**

Do you want Dan Celia to speak to your group or event?
Then email info@FinancialIssues.org.

Whether you want to purchase bulk copies of
*The Fear of Money* or buy another book for a friend,
get it now at www.afastore.afa.net